"Whether we call it magic or folklore (or even superstition), the traditional, often pre-Christian knowledge described in *Pagan Magic of the Northern Tradition* is fascinating. I've been referring to Pennick's books for years when I need a fact or an example of some interesting early magic to cite in my books and blogs. I learned something new on every page!"

BARBARA ARDINGER, PH.D., AUTHOR OF
PAGAN EVERY DAY AND *SECRET LIVES*

"Nigel Pennick is one of the greatest living runic experts, bringing meticulous research and a profound magical understanding to his subject. *Runic Lore and Legend* examines the distinctive Anglo-Saxon Futhark of Northumbria, essentially setting the thirty-three runes in the context of both time and place."

ANNA FRANKLIN, AUTHOR OF *PAGAN WAYS TAROT*

"To have one of the leading authors on the wisdom of the runes pen this comprehensive manual [*Runic Lore and Legend*] on the Northumbrian wyrdstaves is a most valuable gift to all who follow the Northern Tradition. Pennick's weaving of local history and lore around the runes illuminates his subject in a way that no other book has been able to achieve."

RICHARD RUDGLEY, AUTHOR OF *THE RETURN OF ODIN*

"In *Runic Lore and Legend: Wyrdstaves of Old Northumbria,* Pennick delivers the most thorough account of Anglo-Saxon history, mythology, and cosmology. His ability to weave their narrative into the use of the Northumbrian Runes and reveal their modern relevance is nothing less than magickal."

S. KELLEY HARRELL, AUTHOR OF *RUNIC BOOK OF DAYS*

"Nigel Pennick's *Pagan Magic of the Northern Tradition* is a treasure trove of ancient folklore of magical rituals and charms for the protection of people and homes, of barns and livestock, of temples and churches, for good luck and healing as well as causing harm when the rituals are not followed."

NICHOLAS E. BRINK, PH.D., AUTHOR OF *BALDR'S MAGIC: THE POWER OF NORSE SHAMANISM AND ECSTATIC TRANCE*

"*Pagan Magic of the Northern Tradition* offers a well-documented overview of everyday magic, the last recourse against all evils. It introduces us to a strange Pagan world haunted by spirits and supernatural owners of nature and rehabilitates the studies of magic as an important part of our common cultural heritage. Pennick's book is well worth a read!"

CLAUDE LECOUTEUX, PROFESSOR EMERITUS AT THE SORBONNE AND AUTHOR OF *THE TRADITION OF HOUSEHOLD SPIRITS AND DEMONS AND SPIRITS OF THE LAND*

"*The Book of Primal Signs* is a veritable thesaurus of traditional symbolism, spanning from prehistory to today. This is a vital guidebook to a hidden world that is, most thankfully and wondrously, still in plain view."

MICHAEL MOYNIHAN, COAUTHOR OF *LORDS OF CHAOS*

"Solidly referenced and carefully illustrated, *The Book of Primal Signs* seems to travel everywhere and touch everything . . ."

RICHARD HEATH, AUTHOR OF *SACRED NUMBER AND THE ORIGINS OF CIVILIZATION*

Witchcraft &
Secret Societies
of Rural England

The Magic of
TOADMEN, PLOUGH WITCHES,
MUMMERS, AND BONESMEN

Nigel Pennick

Destiny Books
Rochester, Vermont

Destiny Books
One Park Street
Rochester, Vermont 05767
www.DestinyBooks.com

Text stock is SFI certified

Destiny Books is a division of Inner Traditions International

Originally published in the United Kingdom in 2011 by Lear Books under the
    title *In Field and Fen*
First U.S. edition published in 2019 by Destiny Books

Cataloging-in-Publication Data for this title is available from the Library of Congress

ISBN 978-1-62055-760-0 (print)
ISBN 978-1-62055-761-7 (ebook)

Printed and bound in the United States by Lake Book Manufacturing, Inc.
The text stock is SFI certified. The Sustainable Forestry Initiative® program
promotes sustainable forest management.

10 9 8 7 6 5 4 3 2 1

Text design by Debbie Glogover and layout by Priscilla Baker
This book was typeset in Garamond Premier Pro with Heirloom Artcraft and Gill
Sans used as display typefaces

To send correspondence to the author of this book, mail a first-class letter to the
author c/o Inner Traditions • Bear & Company, One Park Street, Rochester, VT
05767, and we will forward the communication.

Contents

Acknowledgments

To those, both living and now departed, for various and sundry assistance over the years, discussions, and information that contributed in one way or another to this book, I thank the following: Ivan Bunn, Michael W. Burgess, Peter Cave, Andrew Chumbley, Michael Clarke, Frances Collinson, Ben Fernee, Anna Franklin, Tony Harvey, Brian Hoggard, Tim Holt-Wilson, Pete Jennings, Patrick McFadzean, Cyril Papworth, Mike Petty, Les Randall, Sid Smith, Val Thomas, John Thorne, Bob Trubshaw, and Genevieve West in addition to the staffs of various libraries, archives, and record offices in Great Britain and Germany.

Keeping Up the Day

Listen, lords, both great and small,
And take good heed of what I say:
I shall you tell as true a tale,
As ever was heard by night or day.

When I watched the demolition of a weather-boarded barn on Bradmore Street, Cambridge, early in 1968, I was struck at how it was going unnoticed that this was the last remaining structure from when that urban street had been farmland. Walking through the rubble, I picked up a smashed pantile, and there, scratched in it by the potter who made it before it went to the kiln, was the date 1738. In 1968, many of the buildings of the town in the Kite area and on the other side of East Road were boarded up in various states of dereliction. Most, unlike the venerable barn, dated from after 1811, when the land had been enclosed and sold off as building plots. Unnoticed and scorned, ready only to be pulled down, many of these buildings had the telltale signs of the craftsmen who made them: stained glass, ornamental weatherboards, wrought-iron wall anchors, doors pierced with the Cambridge "spark of life" pattern. The inhabitants had been moved out, and "sociocide" had taken place so that a new shopping center could be built.

In late 1968, a group of us set up the publication *Cambridge Voice*. It was clear to us that had these buildings been part of the university, they would have been lovingly preserved, and tourists would have taken admiring photographs of them. Although *Cambridge Voice* ceased publication in 1970, in our own small way we attempted to show that the everyday life of the town was authentic, existing with no help from the university, for between town and gown a social apartheid existed that has not changed in all the years since. The identity of Cambridge, as presented to tourists and the world at large, was and is solely of the university, as though the town itself and the working people of the town who serve the university and without whom it could not function were and are of no account. Local identity, important in so many ways, is marginalized within its own home.

To know oneself, one has to know the past. But how we perceive the past is important. The past is not a single thing that can be described and defined like a single object; there is a near-impenetrable complexity in what happened and the effect it has on the present. Many people look back to the past in an uncritical way; there is a tendency to glamorize the past. Reenactors and museum proprietors are in no position to re-create the misery and suffering that characterized large parts of many people's lives in the past, so an acceptable impression is created instead. There is always a tendency to glamorize the past as "the good old days." Some people look back on revisionist versions of history that they present as a golden age. One's golden age depends on one's ideology: ancient Egypt, pagan Ireland, the Baghdad caliphate, Viking Scandinavia, Catholic Christendom, the British Empire, the Soviet Union—all can be presented as wondrous lost worlds where culture flourished and all lives were thereby enriched. How everyday life was for the peasants, artisans, and slaves whose labor kept the caliphs, popes, lords, kings, or party chairmen in luxury is ignored. Others look back more generally, seeking out some utopian societies: tribal, rural, nomadic, religious, national, and so forth. Religious utopians often try to emulate the way of life lived in the early days of the faith, when it was "pure."

Political utopians seek to restore decayed nations and empires. What they all have in common is an understanding that some of the ways of living and doing in the past were of value, but they are lost. By striving to restore the imagined utopias, they are striving to recover the ancient ways represented by their respective utopias.

Unless we are from patrician or aristocratic families whose gene-alogies have been recorded since the Norman Conquest, we do not have much information about our forebears. At best, we may have a few names and the trades they were in at the time certain records were made. But even for the genealogy enthusiast, it is difficult to track down ancestors born before 1800. Though their work sustained the famous who appear in history, they are forgotten. I know that many of my ancestors lived in grinding poverty on the edge of starvation. My ances-tress Elizabeth Hazelwood, who lived, one cannot say "flourished," in Ely in the 1840s, saw most of her children die as babies. Later in the century, things were no better. In 1898 in the *Daily News* was written, "A few years ago, it was the custom to talk and write about 'Derelict Essex' . . . of all the agricultural depression that was to be deplored in England, that of Essex was most hopeless" (*Daily News* 1898). Writing much later, John "Reverend Jack" Putterill, vicar of Thaxted and sup-porter of morris dancing, observed that little of the folk dancing in that part of England was recorded, though it was certainly performed, because the bitter poverty and distress of the nineteenth century had killed it off. Life was unimaginably harsh for the majority who did not have a place in history like their lords and masters.

If I can, through this book, preserve some of the knowledge of all the struggles my ancestors went through, then something of them will live on. Today, these working people, many of whom were barely literate, would be considered ignorant, unpleasant characters. The present-day emphasis on the academic qualifications needful if one is to get a job has marginalized those skills and wisdom embedded within the tradi-tional culture of this country. But, although they are still known about and a few people exercise them, these skills are lost to the majority.

Unfortunately, through this "de-skilling" of society, the greater part of Britain has thrown away the best of our culture. Seeing beyond illusory mundane activities is not encouraged by modernity, obsessed as it is with numbers and finance. Globalized capitalism has no interest in traditions that stretch back to ancient times, preserved and carefully passed down through the generations—unless they can be repackaged for commercial gain. To do so, of course, inevitably destroys their inner essence and the traditions become empty shells devoid of meaning.

The sheer richness of the texture of traditional customs and music in this region is instructional. There is still a real interconnectedness with the activities of everyday life in times before we were dependent on machines and the mass media. Despite everything, many traditional customs have proved very tenacious and continue to be performed. To those who ask why, there are two replies: "It is necessary to keep up the day," and "It's done because it's done." Days kept up by our traditional observances include the summer and winter solstices, Boxing Day (the day after Christmas Day), Twelfth Night, Candlemas, May Day, Lammas, Allhallows' Eve (Hallowe'en), and Martinmas (November 11).

Some traditional practices have continued in individual localities, and so are associated with those places and the county, when, if we but knew it, they may have existed in many other places, too, in the past, but are now undocumented.

These traditions would not exist unless there were people to perform them. Traditionally, the way that they have been kept in being is through groups of people who have some common interest, groups that last longer than the life of any individual. Country customs have been kept going by what came to be called rural fraternities. These range from craft guilds and local trade unions to morris dancers and village bands. Most of the traditions have some elements known only to the people who perform them. These are secrets, often connected with "the tricks of the trade." They are not secret in the way that only members know about them, but they are secrets that can be understood only by those who have in some way been initiated into the group. Practitioners of any secret art must "keep it squat" and conceal it from the view of those who need not know and should not know.

In addition to this necessary secretiveness, there has often been the need to avoid persecution by the religious and civil authorities, and so these organizations were and are compelled to operate clandestinely. This is one reason for the use of masks, face coloring, and other disguises in our tradition. In Scotland, local chapters of the Society of the Horseman's Grip and Word* and lodges of the Oddfellows preserved the old, traditional forms of festivity wherever they could. In this region, it was the Confraternity of the Plough that "kept up the day." Keeping up the day is one of the functions of traditional unadvertised groups whose members make their appearances as broom dancers, plough witches, plough stots, bullockers, boggans, hoodeners, witchmen, and mummers on the wintertime holy days of Tander, Boxing Day, Hogmanay, Twelfth Night, and Plough Monday, and at wassails.† Appearing masked, hooded, in blackface and tatters, as she-males, or guising as the Old Horse, Black Dog, Straw Man, Straw Bear, Crane, Old Sow, and Old Tup, they preserved their anonymity, and in so doing kept the ancient skills and wisdom they held from falling into disuse and extinction, and so have handed them on to us.

As with all things in this transient world, our human culture is ever changing, and its only presence is in its performance. All living cultural traditions, wherever they are, are in a state of continuous evolution, adapting themselves to the particular conditions prevailing at the present moment. This present moment is the result of what has preceded it, that intangible phenomenon that we call the past. There is never a

---

*"Horseman's Word" is the usual East Anglian term: "Horseman's Grip and Word" is the original Scottish form.

†[Because the proper names for Plough Monday and the Confraternity of the Plough use the British spelling of the word *plow,* the British spelling has been retained for this word in all instances. All other words with alternate British spellings have been "Americanized." —*Ed.*]

single cause, never a single answer. But as the Suffolk Horseman and continuator of tradition Neil Lanham once said, "Tradition hangs by a very thin thread." Today, we seek to reflect this regional character, though not necessarily by a literal reproduction of the forms. May the song always be sung again.

NIGEL CAMPBELL PENNICK
MARCH 18, THE DAY OF SAINT EDWARD,
KING AND MARTYR

1

The Geographical Region and Its Links

In field and fen
By pond and pool,
Down by the No-Man's Land,
To the place where all the paths begin
Flow water and blow wind.

ROUTES OF COMMUNICATION

The region this book is about has no name. It contains modern Cambridgeshire, which includes the old Huntingdonshire and the soke of Peterborough, the southern part of Lincolnshire, eastern Northamptonshire and Bedfordshire, northern Essex, part of West Suffolk, and West Norfolk. The main towns of this region are Boston, Cambridge, Huntingdon, King's Lynn, Northampton, and Peterborough. In the old Anglo-Saxon heptarchy, the region was on the borderline between the kingdoms of Mercia and East Anglia, so most of this area is part of East Mercia, the borderlands of the East Midlands, and East Anglia. When this region was under Danish rule, it was part of the Danelaw, but what divisions existed then are no longer apparent. The traditions and folklore of this region are interrelated; they transcend the county boundaries that are used usually to classify them. In the east of this region is a most distinctive landscape—the Fens. Because the county boundaries cross the Fens and parts of the Fens—in Lincolnshire and Huntingdonshire—are not inside the recognized region of East Anglia, the northern part of Fenland tends to be marginalized. Most writings on the Fens concentrate on the southern and middle parts.

The main river across the region is the Great Ouse, whose name is derived from the Celtic word for "water." The river rises at Farthinghoe, to the west of Brackley in Northamptonshire, and it flows through Brackley, Buckingham, Olney, Bedford, St. Neots, Huntingdon, St. Ives, and Ely. Now connected to canals and Fenland drains, it was a major transport route before the rise of rail and highway transport. Huntingdon is an important town in this region, being a major crossing point of the Great Ouse. This river flows into the North Sea via the Wash at King's Lynn. On its course, it has its other main ancient crossing places at Bedford, where in the ninth century the Mercian king Offa was buried in an island chapel, St. Neots, Huntingdon, Godmanchester, and St. Ives. At the last two locations, medieval bridges, still in use, cross the river.

Fig. 1.1. The Great Ouse River and the medieval bridge at St. Ives, Cambridgeshire.

After Holywell, just downstream of St. Ives, where a ferry once operated, the Great Ouse enters the Fens, the farmland that once was swamp interspersed with lakes, where villages and towns were built on islands. From the mid-1500s, the process of progressively draining the Fens began, and in the seventeenth century, the Dutch engineer Cornelis Vermuijden devised and carried out a general scheme to drain the area that became known as the Bedford Level. The main drains built to pump water from the Fens were navigable canals, the most remarkable of which is the dead-straight Old Bedford River that runs from Earith to Denver Sluice, near Downham Market, cutting off the course of the Great Ouse. Here there are two parallel straight canals, the Old and New Bedford Rivers, which can be picked out on satellite photographs of Britain. Between them are the Ouse Washes, in an area intended to flood in the winter to prevent flooding of the adjacent farmland that lies below the river level. The course of the Great Ouse beyond Earith curves to the Isle of Ely and onward to Denver, where the waters of the Bedford Rivers rejoin it. From there, the Great Ouse is

Fig. 1.2. Cattle drover's drift near Dry Drayton, Cambridgeshire.

tidal and runs into the sea past the old Hanseatic port of King's Lynn.

All along the river's length, old roads and tracks run to the riverbanks in places where ferries once operated, and at King's Lynn, the ferry to West Lynn, the oldest continuously operating public transport in Britain, dating back more than seven hundred years, crosses the tidal end of the Great Ouse. The Great Ouse was an important transport link in the days before railways and then road haulage competed with and beat water transport. Many of the Great Ouse's tributary rivers were made navigable, creating a regional water-transport network. Just east of Bedford, the River Ivel was navigable from its junction with the Great Ouse at Tempsford as far as Shefford, but this path was abandoned in 1870. The River Lark was navigable to Bury St. Edmunds until the 1890s. Brandon Creek, north of Ely, was made into a navigable waterway as far as Thetford in the 1700s, but fell out of use during World War I. Almost at King's Lynn, the Great Ouse tributary, the River Nar, was made navigable in the mid-eighteenth century as far as Narborough. Water transport there was abandoned in the 1880s. But in the Fen region of eastern England, until the 1970s, large amounts of material were still transported by water, though the railways had destroyed much of the trade a century earlier.

A tributary to the Great Ouse is the River Cam, which flows through Cambridge. But as the name Cambridge is a truncated, newer form of variants of Grantabridge, the river's name used to be the Granta, Cam being a back formation on the logical deduction that if the town is called Cambridge then the river must be Cam. The River Cam has no spring as its source. It begins at the Weir Pool just above Silver Street Bridge where the Boatyard is. The Granta, coming over the weir, changes its name to the Cam. The name Granta, like Ouse, appears to be of pre-English origin, possibly meaning "shining." Cambridge was a bustling inland port in medieval times. In the areas before the Cam flows into the Great Ouse, several ancient canals, called lodes, provided villages such as Reach, Burwell, and Soham with water transport connections. The Great Ouse itself was connected with other major waterways by various canals and navigations built from the 1600s onward.

Fig. 1.3. Charcoal burners Cook and Bowtle, circa 1890,
with their traditional hut.

Every town on the river had its own hithes and warehouses where goods were transhipped, stored, and distributed and boatyards where boats were built and repaired. From the eighteenth century, there were regular passenger services along this region's rivers, too.

Major connections were made from the Great Ouse when the Fens were drained. From the navigable New Bedford River, a complex of canals known as the Middle Level Navigations were constructed as far west as Peterborough, where they joined with the River Nene. The Nene is the major river in the north of our region, linking Peterborough with Wellingborough and Northampton. Like the Great Ouse, it was a major transport route, having been made navigable between 1724 and 1761. In the twentieth century, the Nene was made deeper and the Dog and Doublet Lock was enlarged, enabling Peterborough to be officially declared an inland port in 1938. Mills were provided with grain brought by barge and bricks were transported from Peterborough Quay.

Fig. 1.4. Collecting osiers in the Fens for basket making, nineteenth century.

The source of the River Nene is near Weedon, a place said to be as far from the sea as it is possible to be in England. The Nene is connected to the narrow boat canal system at Northampton, where the Grand Union Canal joins it. After Wellingborough, it is crossed by a medieval bridge that links Islip with Thrapston; it passes through Oundle before reaching Peterborough, and its canal links into the Fenland waterways. Downstream of Peterborough, the Nene becomes tidal and flows through the old port of Wisbech before entering the Wash. Before the Nene was made navigable with locks, small boats plied the river, being unloaded and dragged overland past difficult sections before being reloaded and going on. In the sixteenth century, the River Nene was navigable as far as Alwalton. Early in the eighteenth century, schemes were drawn up to render the river navigable to Northampton. Navigability between Peterborough and Thrapston was achieved by 1737, and Northampton was able to be visited by transport boats in 1761. From then on until railways were built, heavy transport used the river.

Draining the Fens was undertaken over a period of several hundred years. It was accomplished by digging canals and pumping water into them by wind pumps (called locally windmills). In the nineteenth century, steam-pumping stations replaced the major windmills, and later gas or petrol engines and finally diesels took over the pumps. Perhaps because Dutch engineers were employed in draining the Fens,

Fig. 1.5. Isaac Garratt, a Fenman known as King of the Fisherman for his feat of catching a sturgeon six feet and seven inches long and weighing 112 pounds in the Great Ouse River on Whit Monday 1816. Etching by William Johnstone White, 1818. The Library of the European Tradition.

these windmills were all named, as is the custom in the Netherlands. The chief market towns along the rivers all had wharves at which the barges, called lighters in this region, were loaded and unloaded. Close to the wharves were warehouses, mills, breweries, workshops, boatyards, foundries, and inns where business was conducted. River transport was by far the best means of carrying goods in the days before decent roads were made. The present-day prevalence of road transport makes us perceive local geography from a different perspective than that in the past. Markets and industries using bulk goods were invariably near navigable rivers or canals in the days before railways. The great fairs in Cambridge, the Midsummer Fair and the Sturbridge Fair, were held in fields next to the River Cam. The largest flour mills in the region were water powered, and grain was brought by water. Toward the end of the nineteenth century, coal was brought by water to fire the new electric power stations, and sugar beets were transported by water to the regional sugar factories of the early twentieth century.

The rivers provided a link with other parts of England and, through their connections with the coast, with seaborne routes to other parts of

Britain and mainland Europe. On the land, roads were poor because there was no national strategic network funded by a central government. Even long-distance roads were repaired by local effort, and, as is usual today, things that cost money were done on the cheap or not at all. Wheeled transport was the least attractive of all forms. However, transport, though slow and difficult by twenty-first-century standards, was effective by non-wheeled means. Peddlers walked trackways, carrying their wares on their back, while packhorses carried heavier goods in panniers, trekking along narrow pathways through the land. "The ubiquity of the Scotch packman produced the sign of the *Scotchman's Pack*," wrote Larwood and Hotten in their comprehensive book on British signboards. There is documentary evidence that Scottish packmen traveled as far as Poland (Larwood and Hotten 1908, 421–22). Herds of animals were also driven for long distances, often across country or on roads unfit for wheels.

Larwood and Hotten also note the connection of inns with traditional means of transport without wheels.

> The *Drover's Call* is still seen on many roadsides, though the profession that gave rise to it is well-nigh extinct; the herds of steaming, fierce-looking oxen, formerly driven from all parts of the kingdom,

Fig. 1.6. Draining Whittlesea Mere, a lake of several square miles' area, which was pumped dry using steam power in the mid-nineteenth century. This engraving shows Appold's Pump. The livelihoods of local Fen fishermen and waterfowl hunters were thereby destroyed, and they were forced to become laborers, tilling the soil for the new owners of the lake bed. The Library of the European Tradition.

Fig. 1.7. Laborers draining the Fens. Etching by William Johnstone White, 1818. The Library of the European Tradition.

along the main roads leading to London, there to be devoured, being now nearly all sent here by rail. A yet older practice produced the sign of the *String of Horses,* which may still be seen on many a high-road in the North, and dates from times before mail coaches and stage waggons existed, when all the goods-traffic inland had to be performed by strings of packhorses, who carried large baskets, hampers, and bales slung across their backs, and slowly, though far from surely, wound their way over miles and miles of uninhabited tracts, moors, and fens, which lay between the small towns and straggling villages. (Larwood and Hotten 1908, 355)

After the English Civil War, from the 1650s, droving of cattle long distances in Britain became an important business. Cattle from Scotland were driven southward into England on their way to the markets and slaughterhouses of Smithfield to feed the people of London, or indirectly via East Anglia, where the cattle were sold to local stockmen who fattened them before driving them to London along the drovers' road via Chelmsford. By the time they had reached this region, the majority of drovers were driving their herds down the Great North Road at Alconbury

Hill, which is still a major traffic point to this day, at the junction of the
A1 motorway and the northern spur of the A14. At Alconbury Hill, the
Old North Road, otherwise called the Old Post Road, which runs via
Huntingdon and Royston, left the Great North Road. The Great North
Road took the herds southward through Hertfordshire to Barnet, where
a famous fair was held, and the last stop before London was Highgate,
where the drovers' custom of Swearing on the Horns, derived from the
drovers' initiation, is maintained. The Bull and Last Inn there was the
last stopping place for drovers before Smithfield. The parallel Old North
Road entered London via Shoreditch.

Cattle and sheep from Wales also found their way into this region via
two Welsh drovers' roads. One, from North Wales, came to Northampton
via Brownhills. The other, which started at Builth Wells and followed
Banbury Lane from Banbury to Northampton, crossing the Welsh Road
at Culworth, then by way of the regional hub, Huntingdon, brought livestock to be sold in the markets at St. Ives, Setchey, near King's Lynn, or at
the great Saint Faith's Fair near Norwich, where the Scottish drovers also

Fig. I.8. Oxen used in transport, eighteenth century.
The Library of the European Tradition.

took most of their herds. Some of the cattle driven by Welsh and Scottish drovers to this region had originated in Ireland.

ISOLATION AND COMMUNICATION

Folklore collectors in the nineteenth century rescued much of our culture from oblivion, so we are grateful that this rich tradition was not allowed to disintegrate and be lost. They wrote down lore, songs, and dances that existed in their areas, and often categorized them as specifically unique to that place. But despite the settled populations in rural areas, their culture was ever open to new influences from elsewhere. Regular travelers crossed the region, interacting with the inhabitants. Journeymen and tradesmen "on the tramp" looking for work could find it if they knew the grips and words of their fraternity, for the knowledge was within their craft wherever they went. The ever-traveling Romani were famed as musicians and brought tunes and songs; they also told fortunes and transmitted magical knowledge. Peddlers carried necessities and also sold publications that disseminated everything from music to medical remedies. So although a person may not have traveled outside her village in her lifetime, she still had access to a wide range of culture, lore, and legend that did not come from her home area. However, traditional local culture in arable and livestock-rearing parts of the region remained the mainstream to which new elements were added where they fitted.

Out in the Fens, people were far more isolated. Until well into the twentieth century, the heyday of police activity, there was little policing, and even today, remote parts of the area are thinly policed. Activities that had been suppressed in more accessible places were carried on in the Fens. For example, at Upware in the 1860s, the Five Miles from Anywhere, No Hurry was a public house where bargemen held "prize fights," illegal bare-fist boxing matches. Students came there from Cambridge by boat to escape the strictures of university regulation and formed the Upware Republic, a fellowship dedicated to binge drinking. On the Great Ouse, in the 1940s, the isolated Brownshill Lock had a

Fig. 1.9. A local tradition kept up today is broom dancing, a skilled art still taught to new generations. The Mepal Molly Men dancing at Whittlesea, January 12, 2008.

pub kept by the lock keeper. It was far away from the law, so observed no licensing hours.

Molly dancing survived in the Fens when it had been suppressed elsewhere* as did dog fighting. Fenland handywomen continued to practice mercy killing until 1902. The cultivation of hemp (cannabis) for hemp tea, banned around 1920, was never quite eliminated in the Fens, where the opium poppy also provided a harvest. Hemp tea was a sovereign remedy for the ague, the endemic illness of the mosquito-infested Fens, and until the First World War, opic (opium) pills were sold by peddlers to pub regulars to take along with a beer chaser. The proper use of these substances was part of the traditional knowledge of handywomen and witches. Hallowe'en, which by 1940 had almost died out as a festival in other parts of Britain, was observed in the Fens, where witchcraft was practiced and feared. The Fens remain the spiritual home of toadmanry, and the Bonesmen, too. The last recorded horse-skull foundation deposit in England, under a new Primitive Methodist chapel, also took place in the Fens at Black Horse Drove.

---

*The newly founded police force decided molly dancing was begging and hence illegal. Constables in towns were sent out on Plough Monday to arrest any dancers in their traditional disguise. In the remote fens, where the police never went, there was no one to stop the dancers.

In the early nineteenth century, the invention of steam-powered transport, especially on rails, led to new, regular, rapid transport across the whole land. Run from London and bringing metropolitan culture to the countryside, the railways altered the cultural qualities of the countryside. Gradually, the predominant culture became the urban, accelerated by the compulsory schooling of children after 1870. In Wales, the schools attempted to stop the speaking of Welsh by the notorious "Welsh Not" sign and by beating children who persisted. Local beliefs and traditions of this part of England were condemned by schoolteachers who tried to indoctrinate children with the recommended values. The introduction of the radio and other electronic media further accelerated the downgrading of local tradition, which now was derided as rural and unfashionable. Mainstream culture became, and remains, that of the mass media, with local, traditional ways having become a kind of counterculture. But despite deliberate attempts and accidental unintended consequences, traditional culture, including the magical tradition, has not been completely extirpated. The secrets of the countryside still remain; the rites and ceremonies are still conducted in "keeping up the day," and some of the mysterious rural fraternities still meet and initiate new members. We shall meet some of them further on.

Fig. 1.10. Traditional warding signs are present as cutouts on the window shutters of this house in Melbourn, Cambridgeshire.

2

The Drovers

THE BUSINESS OF DROVING

Cattle and sheep have been herded across the British countryside for thousands of years, and by the medieval period, flourishing businesses existed, driving herds of animals long distances. One of the earliest surviving documents of droving is *The Diary of a Drover's Month,* which describes a mixed herd of cattle and sheep driven from Long Sutton in Lincolnshire to Tadcaster in Yorkshire in May 1323, a distance of 230 kilometers. Scottish drovers were taking animals southward through England as early as 1359. Throughout the period when droving took place, there were many hazards to contend with. Until the eighteenth century in wilder areas, wolves threatened to kill straggling members of the herd. Bands of outlaws and brigands and later, highwaymen, were always on the lookout for anyone carrying large sums of money.

Droving was a trade that continued for more than six hundred years, so as with all trades and crafts, there was a body of lore and techniques dealing with the eldritch side of life. Some drovers used a dried bull's penis as a staff to drive their cattle. Most drovers carried sticks of rowan because they believed it to be foolhardy to undertake a journey without one. According to British magical tradition, rowan, otherwise called mountain ash or quickentree, is an amulet that wards off evil

Fig. 2.1. Traditional Fenland house at Over, Cambridgeshire.

spirits and bewitchments and also prevents accidents. An old Scottish rhyme describes the rowan charm.

> *Rowan tree and red threid,*
> *Gar the witches tyne their speed.*
> [Rowan tree and red thread,
> make the witches lose their speed
> (effectiveness)].

At the same time as they were carrying magical amulets and talismans to aid the journey and protect the herd, drovers also observed Christian strictures. Sunday observance was strictly enforced, and there were heavy penalties for walking cattle on a Sunday. Some Welsh drovers were known for their religious piety, and some are known to have composed hymns on their droving journeys. The Welsh drover Dafydd Jones, who frequented the cattle fairs at Barnet and

Maidstone, translated the hymns of Isaac Watts into Welsh (Toulson 1980, 9). But secular songs were more common than hymns, and drovers had particular work songs that they sang as they traveled the moors, drifts, and roads. Some Scots drovers who played the bagpipes would encourage weary herds by playing special tunes to them. These songs were sung and their tunes played in the inns where the drovers stopped for the night. Undoubtedly, tunes popular in Scotland were picked up by local musicians in the areas through which the drovers passed.

In his story "The Two Drovers," Sir Walter Scott gives a description of the trade of droving at the beginning of the nineteenth century.

> Many large droves were about to set off for England, under the protection of their owners, or of the topsmen whom they employed in the tedious, laborious, and responsible office of driving the cattle for many hundred miles, from the market where they had been purchased, to the fields or farmyards where they were to be fattened for the shambles. The Highlanders in particular are masters of this difficult trade of driving, which seems to suit them as well as the trade of war. It affords exercise for all their habits of patient endurance and active exertion. They are required to know perfectly the drove-roads, which lie over the wildest tracts of the country, and to avoid as much as possible the highways, which distress the feet of the bullocks, and the turnpikes, which annoy the spirit of the drover; whereas on the broad green or grey track, which leads across the pathless moor, the herd not only move at ease and without taxation, but, if they mind their business, may pick up a mouthful of food by the way. At night, the drovers usually sleep along with their cattle, let the weather be what it will; and many of these hardy men do not once rest under a roof during a journey on foot from Lochaber to Lincolnshire. They are paid very highly, for the trust reposed is of the last importance, as it depends on their prudence, vigilance and honesty, whether the cattle reach the final market in good order,

and afford a profit to the grazier. But as they maintain themselves at their own expense, they are especially economical in that particular.

Scott says that the drovers would not take their cattle on the drove "without tying Saint Mungo's knot on their tails" to ward off witchcraft. "It may not be indifferent to the reader to know that the Highland cattle are peculiarly liable to be taken, or infected, by spells and witchcraft, which judicious people guard against by knitting knots of peculiar complexity on the tuft of hair which terminates the animal's tail" (Scott 2018).

Drovers from Scotland crossed this region, driving large herds of cattle on their way to the regional markets and farther southward to the slaughterers at Smithfield in London. There were many routes farther north, the tracks and roads taken in the northerly parts depending on whether the drovers were coming from the cattle fair of the Falkirk Tryst or farther west from Dumfries. There were two main ways to enter London, by the Great North Road or the Old North Road, otherwise called the Old Post Road. The two roads separated at Alconbury Hill, north of Huntingdon. The milestone at Alconbury Hill read, "To London 64 miles through Huntingdon Royston and Ware," while on the other side was carved, "To London 68 miles through Buckden Biggleswade and Hatfield." These are statute miles of eight furlongs, still in use in the twenty-first century, not the old customary miles of ten furlongs, sometimes called country miles or long miles, which traditionally were used by drovers and packmen.

The Great North Road took the westerly route southward through Biggleswade, Baldock, Stevenage, Welwyn, Hatfield, and Barnet, where a major fair for the sale of livestock was held. Barnet Fair was a place where both cattle and horses were sold and bought, visited by both Scots and Welsh drovers. Its fame survives linguistically in Cockney rhyming slang, which talks about a person's "barnet": Barnet Fair = hair. From Barnet, the route passed through Highgate, along the Holloway Road, Upper Street Islington, and thence joining with the easterly route along Saint John's Street to Smithfield. Highgate retains the drovers' ritual of Swearing on the Horns, used in later years by the landlord of the Gate

House Tavern as a means of getting travelers to stand drinks all round. The Bull and Last Inn at Highgate was the final drovers' stopping place before reaching Smithfield.

Huntingdon, bypassed by the Great North Road, was the objective of some Scottish drovers. The Midsteeple in Dumfries, a stone tower at the center of the town, served as a milestone for Scottish drovers who gathered there. Among other drovers' destinations in England listed on the Midsteeple are "Huntingdon 272 miles. London 330 miles." Just north of Huntingdon, from Alconbury Hill, the Old North Road takes the more easterly route southward, by way of Huntingdon, Caxton, Royston, Ware, Hoddesdon, Enfield Highway, Stamford Hill, Kingsland, Shoreditch, and Islington before arriving at Smithfield, sixty-four miles from Alconbury Hill.

Drovers from Wales also came across this region. There was a flourishing trade in cattle from Wales to England as early as the middle of

Fig. 2.2. A Smithfield drover with his London registration number worn on a plate on his arm. W. H. Pyne, 1808. The Library of the European Tradition.

the thirteenth century, and gaps in Offa's Dyke on old roads that are known to have been drovers' routes in later years indicate cattle droving in the eighth century. By the middle of the seventeenth century, the cattle trade with England was essential to the economy of Wales. Industrialization and urban growth in the second half of the eighteenth century greatly increased the demand for beef from the graziers of the Midlands and East Anglia. This greatly increased the droving of cattle both from Wales and Scotland into these regions, as well as to London, where Smithfield was where many cattle were sold and slaughtered.

Coming out of Wales along the Welsh Road (otherwise called the Welshman's Road) from Wrexham and Whitchurch, some drovers took their cattle to the stopping place of the Rising Sun at Brownhills in Staffordshire. Some then brought their droves to Northampton and beyond by way of Watling Street. Others, coming on a more southerly route, came to Northampton via the ancient green trackway called Banbury Lane, which begins near Chipping Norton at the Rollright Stones, coming through Banbury to Northampton. Some Welsh cattle were sold at the markets at Northampton, Daventry, Market Harborough, Leicester, Rugby, and Uppingham to be put out to graze locally. Spratton, near Northampton, was the most important market of Welsh cattle at the end of the droving era. Those not sold in that region were driven farther eastward through Bedford into Essex to be sold at fairs at Harlow Bush, Braintree, Chelmsford, Brentwood, and Romford. In his book *Wild Wales,* published in 1854, George Borrow described a Welsh drover called Mr. Bos and his modus operandi.

The oldest known reference to the Welsh Road is from 1758 in the Enclosure Award for Helmdon. There are a number of evocative place-names along this road. There is Welshman's Hill near Castle Bromwich, Welsh Meadow near Halesowen, and between Offchurch and Prior's Hardick, there are Welsh Road Bridge, Welsh Road Farm, Welsh Road Gorse, and Welsh Road Meadow. Near Culworth, the Welsh Road is crossed by another important Welsh drovers' route—Banbury Lane. This is a continuation of the drovers' route that comes from the crossing point of the River Severn, the Aust Passage (Drew, 738–43).

In the East Midlands, the fairs and markets at Northampton, Leicester, and Market Harborough were significant primary objectives of the Welsh drovers traveling the byway of the Welsh Road or Banbury Lane. They preferred to sell at these major trading centers unless prices were better at the smaller fairs in the localities. From 1840 Spratton was a major collecting point for cattle droves bound for the larger centers and destined for the various markets of the English Midlands. The trade was so large that, in the 1860s, Welsh dealers acquired 149 acres of land there to hold cattle until favorable times for their sale. The importance of Northampton as a center of the cattle trade can be seen from the Welsh drover Rhys Morgan of Tregaron, who traded in horses and cattle until the early twentieth century and was called "the King of Northampton." Large amounts of leather were required by the shoemakers in Northampton, and driven cattle slaughtered in the town provided their skins to the local tanners who supplied the craftsmen.

Until the late nineteenth century and in some cases into the twentieth, Welsh drovers brought their cattle into the midland and southeastern counties of England. By then their chief objectives were the November Fair at Hertford and Barnet Fair. The latter was widely recognized as the major gathering place for the drovers from Wales. In October 1856, a description of Barnet Fair, very disparaging of the Welsh drovers for not speaking English, was published in *The Farmers' Magazine.*

Imagine some hundreds of bullocks like an immense forest of horns, propelled hurriedly towards you amid the hideous and uproarious shouting of a set of semi-barbarous drovers who value a restive bullock far beyond the life of a human being, driving their mad and noisy herds over every person they meet if not fortunate enough to get out of their way; closely followed by a drove of unbroken wild Welsh ponies, fresh from their native hills, all of them loose and unrestrained as the oxen that preceded them; kicking, rearing and biting each other . . . lots of "un-English speaking" Welshmen who may have just sold some of their native bovine stock whilst they are to be seen throwing up their long-worn, shapeless hats high in the air, as a type of Taffy's delight, uttering at the same time a trade of gibberish which no-one can understand but themselves.

Turnpike tolls were a significant cost for the drovers from Wales. Each animal had to be paid for, meticulously counted through the toll-gate one by one. So although turnpike roads were more direct and a quicker way to drive animals to market, they were also costly to use, and some drovers would take their droves longer distances across country to avoid paying tolls. In 1859, *The Hereford Journal* noted "the great abhorrence of the Radnorshire men for a tollgate." Only twenty years before that, in Wales, the resentment against the "toll farmers" who ran the turnpike tollgates, charging excessively, had led to the Rebecca Riots, which had threatened to become a revolution. In George Sturt's *A Farmer's Life,* John Smith says of the Welsh drovers going to the fairs at Blackwater and Farnham, "They'd lose a day goin' round sooner'n they'd pass a gate" (Sturt 1927, 19).

An understanding of the nature of the landscape was necessary for the drovers' trade. The ability to deal with difficult places and bring the animals through unscathed was a necessary skill. Beasts had to be driven through narrow rocky passes, across hazardous summits, through rivers, and swum across estuaries. Difficult points on roads and trackways—places of passage—are places where spiritual assistance is necessary. The Saint Mungo's knot in the tail protected the animal not only from bewitchment but also the hazards of passage. In the days before bridges, fording a river was a hazardous, possibly life-threatening, necessity. A shrine before a ford allowed the wayfarer to call on the spirits to allow him or her to cross the river, then once crossed successfully, to give thanks for a safe passage. Passes through mountains, marked by cairns of memory and thanksgiving, are similar.

DROVERS' LANDSCAPE MARKERS

When one travels through the landscape of England and Wales today, one often comes across small groups of pine trees standing isolated from other trees. These are always Scots pines (*Pinus sylvestris*), which grow closely together. Not far from where I am writing this, at a junction of major trunk roads, stands such a group, three living trees and one that is now only standing deadwood. Along the routes where the herds passed were farms where the drovers could pasture animals overnight to feed, for a payment to the farmer. Many inns stood close by where drovers would stay the night. These stopping places were usually marked by clumps of Scots pines, visible from considerable distances in open country. In a few places, other kinds of notable tree were planted as stance markers. On the chalklands in the south, yews were mark trees, and at Naphill Common near High Wycombe, a rare Portuguese laurel marked the stance (Toulson 1980, 28).

These notable clumps of pine trees have been of no interest to archaeologists as they cannot be classified as individual "sites" worthy of documentation and study. Likewise, they were not taken notice of by countryside preservationists because they were just trees, seemingly like any other. The groups of pines were actually planted as markers

Fig. 2.3. Stance or clump of Scots pine trees, planted as markers for drovers driving their herds cross-country. In Cambridgeshire, these clumps, most of which have now been cut down, were called "the Devil's Plantation."

Fig. 2.4. Scottish drovers in an inn, circa 1870. The Library of the European Tradition.

on trackways and roads, but not to mark straightness in the landscape, as Alfred Watkins, the Old Straight Track man, speculated.

The railways put an end to long-distance droving of herds across the land. It became cheaper to herd the animals into cattle cars and send them to market than to drive them across country. The railways also blocked many of the traditional drovers' roads, called drifts, thus hindering or preventing cattle drives, and the clumps of pine trees lost their meaning except as memorials of a bygone way of life.

OX SHOEING

As with some plough teams of oxen working hard land, cattle to be driven long distances along roads were shod with iron cattle shoes called cues. Unlike horses, whose feet can be lifted one at a time to take the horseshoe, cattle must be laid down on the ground. "Few smiths, though they can shoe a horse well, are able to shoe an ox . . . ," wrote John Tuke in 1801. "The feet of the ox being drawn together with strong ropes, they are always cast or thrown down, which is sometimes attended by accidents" (Tuke 1801, 255). Throwing the ox was a skilled art, from which the drovers' initiations at Highgate, Hoddesdon, and Ware derived the term "taking the bull by the horns." One blacksmith could shoe seventy head of cattle a day. Because cattle have cloven hooves, each animal needs to have eight cues, crescent-shaped iron plates fastened with nails like horseshoes, between three and five nails per cue. These nails were forged crooked and stored like that until needed. Thus, the scale that forms on handmade nails was left as a protective coating until the nail was needed, when an apprentice hammered it straight, knocking off the scale. Then the nails were thrust into a piece of fat pork before being hammered in to lubricate the nail and make it go in more easily and prevent it from rusting. Tuke described the shoeing of oxen: "The shoes are thin and broad, covering a great part of the foot, and rather turning up at the toe between the hoofs, they are fastened with broad flat-headed nails, covering with their heads a great part of the shoe" (Tuke 1801, 255).

There was a return trade in cues taken from animals slaughtered at Smithfield in London. They were sorted for reusable cues, which were transported north again, and the others taken by blacksmiths for recycling. In the early twentieth century, hundreds of cattle shoes were excavated outside the Travellers' Rest, an inn on the old Godmanchester Turnpike, northwest of Cambridge, now the Huntingdon Road, just at the present city boundary (Glover 1960, 219–20). The last shoeing of oxen in England continued long after long-distance droving ended. Until World War II, the Atora Suet Company used bullock carts for their publicity value. The "six brown-and-white steers pulling a wagon" toured the country, and occasionally local blacksmiths were called on to reshoe the oxen. A news photograph taken in Sunderland in 1935 shows the cues well (Boyle 1983, 26). Wags Aldred records how in Ipswich on the way to Martlesham, an Atora ox lost a shoe, and blacksmith Les Finch was called on to provide a new one. Afterward, he hung the old cues in his travis to prove he was a versatile blacksmith who had shod bullocks (Aldred, n.d., 36–38).

PACKHORSE TRAINS

Packhorse gangs were a common form of long-distance transport throughout the British Isles in the seventeenth and eighteenth centuries before the construction of turnpike roads, canals, wagonways, tramroads, and railways. A train was a number of horses of a gang proceeding in single file, led by a lead horse fitted with bells. Each horse in the train was fitted with packs or panniers supported by a wooden saddle. Packhorse trains crossed the land along direct trackways or across open moorland by customary routes that the drovers also used. They avoided the circuitous lanes linking farmsteads and villages, for in this time most of the land was held in common and had not been appropriated by aristocratic landowners through the Parliamentary process called enclosure, which was seen by some as legalized theft in realty. The bells on the lead horse served as a marker for the other horses to follow.

For example, in his *History of Quadrupeds,* published in Newcastle upon Tyne in 1790, Thomas Bewick noted that the packhorses, "in their journeys over the trackless moors . . . strictly adhere to the line of order and regularity custom has taught them to observe; the leading Horse, which is always chosen for his sagacity and steadiness, being furnished with bells, gives notice to the rest, which follow the sound, and generally without much deviation, though sometimes at a considerable distance" (Bewick 1790). The bells on the lead horse also gave notice to other travelers that a packhorse train was coming, and they could take avoiding action.

According to a Horseman's Society catechism, Bell and Star were the names of the first tame mare and the first tame stallion (*Society of the Horseman's Grip and Word* 2009). The bell is linked with the star as both are symbols of guidance. The bell on the lead horse guides the packhorse train. The leading star, known in eastern England as the Nowl and to astronomers as Polaris, the Pole Star, always stays in the same place over the North Pole and thus permits navigation at sea and on land.

Because transport using animals is scarcely known anymore in the British Isles, it is important to recognize that all animals were trained in the past. Up until the middle of the twentieth century, the delivery of milk and coal in British cities was done by horse-drawn cart or milk float. The horses knew their rounds and would walk to the next stopping place without being driven by the roundsman, a significant advantage over a vehicle that must be climbed into each time it must be moved. An advertisement that appeared in the *Leeds Mercury* in 1728 had for sale "a gang of good Pack Horses, containing eighteen in number with their accoutrements and Business, belonging to the same, being one of the ancient Gangs that has gone with Goods from York, Leeds and Wakefield to London, being the Horses of Thomas Varley; whoever hath mind to buy them may apply" (*Leeds Mercury* 1728).

In the packhorse trains, the horses knew their routes and would follow them even if the packman was not with them. Packmen would stop off at a traveler's rest to have a pint of ale while the horses in the train proceeded by themselves. Then, after refreshment, he would ride on to join them for a while and then go ahead to his next stopping place. Meanwhile, the horses continued along their accustomed route toward their destination. Horses pulling barges and lighters on the Great Ouse River also knew what to do. When they came to low fences that blocked the haling way (towpath), they were trained to jump them. The horse knew how long to wait before jumping so there would be enough slack rope to get over the fence (Simper circa 2000, 57).

Similarly, drovers' dogs made their way across country unaccompanied. Scottish drovers who had successfully brought their herds to sale in England sometimes sent their dogs back home ahead of them. The dogs knew the way they had come, stopping at farms and inns where they were fed. The drover, returning after them, paid for their food, and the dogs arrived home early, letting the drover's family know that he was on the way back to Scotland. Philip Gwyn Hughes tells of a dog called Carlo who accompanied his master, a Welsh drover, from Wales to Kent and then went back by the same route before the drover, completing the journey in a week (Hughes 1943).

3

Markets and Fairs

THE STURBRIDGE FAIR

The goals of drovers' journeys were the many markets and fairs held along their routes where they could sell their animals for a good price. Near Cambridge, on what is now called Stourbridge Common, was a great fair that finally closed down in the 1930s. Sturbridge Common, where the fair was set up, was the remains of the much larger medieval field of Estenhale in the Barnwell district of Cambridge, part of the site of a great fair variously called the Stirbitch, Sturbridge, or Stourbridge Fair. The brickmakers nearby put the name Sturbridge on their products, so I shall use this spelling, which coincides with the proper pronunciation of the place-name, for the fair.

Like the other great Cambridge fair, the Midsummer Fair, held on Midsummer Common, the Sturbridge Fair was also given a charter during the reign of King John, in 1211 (Mitchell 1985, 4). The River Cam flows along one side of Sturbridge Common, as it does Midsummer Common a mile upstream, so in the days when commodities were carried best long-distance by river vessels, it was a convenient place to deliver goods. A 1589 charter stated that it "far surpassed the greatest of and most celebrated fairs of all England; whence great benefits had resulted to the merchants of the whole kingdom, who resorted thereto, and there quickly sold their wares and merchandises to purchasers coming from all parts of the Realm" (Taylor 1999, 113–20). The 1607 edition of William Camden's *Britannia* called it "the most famous fair in all England." From 1651, the construction of Denver Sluice meant that seagoing ships could no longer navigate to Cambridge, so goods had to be transhipped at King's Lynn onto barges known as fen lighters. Denver Sluice was out of action from 1717, when it was destroyed by an exceptional high tide, to 1749, when it was rebuilt. It is likely that seagoing vessels came to Sturbridge during this period. Fen lighters were used thereafter until the demise of trading at the fair in the middle of the nineteenth century.

Daniel Defoe visited Sturbridge Fair on his journey round Great Britain that he published in letter 1 part 3 in the first volume of *A Tour through the Whole Island of Great Britain*. Some have claimed

Fig. 3.1. Market traders, 1818. Formerly, it was customary for men and women to carry items on their heads in England. Etching by William Johnstone White, 1818. The Library of the European Tradition.

that at that time it was the largest fair in Europe. The Sturbridge Fair was certainly a center of distribution of goods and a meeting place for long-distance travelers. Though much of the goods came by water, packhorses carrying wool from Kendal took fifteen days on the road to reach Sturbridge Common. Defoe described the variety of textile goods on sale at the fair.

> Here are clothiers from Halifax, Leeds, Wakefield and Huddersfield in Yorkshire, and from Rochdale, Bury, etc., in Lancashire, with vast quantities of Yorkshire cloths, kerseys, pennistons, cottons, etc., with all sorts of Manchester ware, fustians, and things made of cotton wool; of which the quantity is so great, that they told me there were near a thousand horse-packs of such goods from that side of the country, and these took up a side and half of the Duddery at least; also a part of a street of booths were taken up with upholsterer's ware, such as tickings, sackings, Kidderminster stuffs, blankets, rugs, quilts, etc. In the Duddery I saw one warehouse, or booth with six apartments in it, all belonging to a dealer in Norwich stuffs only, and who, they said, had there above twenty thousand pounds value in those goods, and no other. Western goods had their share here also, and several booths were filled as full with serges, duroys, druggets, shalloons, cantaloons, Devonshire kerseys, etc., from Exeter, Taunton, Bristol, and other parts west, and some from London also. (Defoe 1724)

This was then one of the largest fairs in England, yet in 1723 Defoe noted, "In a word, the fair is like a well-fortified city, and there is the least disorder and confusion I believe, that can be seen anywhere with so great a concourse of people." It was said at that time that men from London came to the fair not to do business but to "drink, smoke, and whore," as though that was not easily done in London without having to make an expensive and perilous road journey to Sturbridge Common and back again. So the disapproving puritan John Bunyan used Sturbridge Fair as the model for Vanity Fair in his *The Pilgrim's Progress,* in turn inspiring William Makepeace Thackeray to write *Vanity Fair.*

One of the most important commodities traded at Sturbridge Fair was hops. The fair served as the national market and set the going price for the year. The hops themselves were grown mainly in Kent and Surrey and were sold to the brewers from Ware in Hertfordshire, and some were bought from brewers from the north (Nichols 1786, 72). Large flocks of up to five hundred geese at a time were driven from Suffolk and Norfolk to Sturbridge to be sold there (Knight 1859, 32). In 1772, the writer Charles Caraccioli noted that "the shops or booths are built in regular rows like streets, having each their name." According to Caraccioli, it was "the greatest temporary mart in the world" (Caraccioli 1772, 19). The main row was Garlic Row, occupied in the late eighteenth century by jewelers, silversmiths, ironmongers, and hardware stalls. The booths were substantial prefabricated constructions, stored at the nearby Barnwell Leper Chapel when not in use. Garlic Row remains as a Cambridge street, as does Oyster Row. In an account of the fair published in *The Mirror of Literature, Amusement and Instruction* in 1828, William Hone, who went by his fair name Nimble Heels or the Greek ΣΗΝΥΑ, stated that the oysters came from the Lynn Channel at King's Lynn, were the size of a horse's hoof, and were opened with a pair of pincers. Oyster shells may still be picked up on Stourbridge Common and found in the river, along with fragments of clay pipes, when it is dredged. The center of the fair was an open square called the Duddery, which measured between 240 and 300 feet along each side. At the center was a tall maypole (it was called that) with a wind vane at the top. The minister of Barnwell conducted religious services in the Duddery on the two main Sundays during the fair.

Writing in 1827, Hone shared his personal recollections of the fair in the 1760s: "The importance of the Stirbitch fair may be estimated by the great extent of ground it occupied. The circuit of the fair, beginning at the first show booth round by the cheese fair, the wool fair, and hop fair; then onwards to Ironmongers' row, to the horse fair; northward on

Fig. 3.2. Booth at the Sturbridge Fair, Barnwell, Cambridge, circa 1820. The Library of the European Tradition.

to the pottery fair, along the margin of the Cam, by the coal fair; then southward to the outside of the Inn, and proceeding in a direct line by the basket fair to the point whence you started made full three miles" (Hone 1827, 1548).

Periodic attempts were made by the university authorities to prohibit plays and other activities at the Sturbridge Fair, as in a 1592 decree that banned the performance of all plays within five miles of Cambridge. A royal charter granted by James I in the 1600s had given the vice-chancellor of Cambridge University powers to "prohibit idle games and diversions" and to "expel jugglers and actors" (Porter 1969, 138–39). But like most laws, they were poorly policed and largely ineffective. But by the end of the eighteenth century, the fair sported two theaters. John Gay's *The Beggar's Opera* was performed there in 1767.

Caraccioli records in 1753 "buildings for the exhibition of drolls, puppet shows, legerdemain, mountebanks, wild beasts, monsters, giants, dwarfs, rope dancers etc" (Caraccioli 1772).

Justice, or punishment, was meted out by the Court of Pie Powder, a court of summary jurisdiction whose name derived from *pieds poudreux,* "dusty feet." George Williamson notes the late survival of these courts well into the twentieth century at Sturbridge Fair, at Cambridge, at Modbury, and at the Bridge Fair at Peterborough, though F. J. Drake-Carnell writes (inaccurately) of the courts surviving in 1938 at Newcastle, Sturbridge Fair, and Guildford. Gypsies were whipped at the fair in 1602 for practicing palmistry. A pamphlet attributed to Ned Ward called *A Step to Stir-Bitch Fair,* published in Cambridge in 1700, tells that the district was called Bawdy-Barnwell, "so-called from the numerous Brothel-Houses that it contains for the health, ease and pleasure of the Learned vicinity." The fair contained "a multitude of gentry, scholars, tradesmen, whores, hawkers, pedlars and pick-pockets."

The fair was related to the harvest season, being proclaimed on September 7 each year, and after the change of the calendar in 1752, to September 16. If the harvest had not been gathered in, the stall holders were permitted to set up on the unharvested crops. On the last day of the fair, sports such as horse racing, running, and wrestling took place. On Michaelmas Day at noon (after 1752, Old Michaelmas Day), the ploughmen were permitted to enter and begin ploughing up Stourbridge Common, whether or not the last stall keepers had packed up and left. Anything not taken away by then was forfeit to the farmers. Winter ploughing took place between Michaelmas and Christmas, and spring ploughing between Plough Monday and Lady Day.

THE STURBRIDGE INITIATION

"From the earliest times countrymen have handed down a series of initiations of which only mutilated fragments remain," wrote Leslie F. Newman, "but there is enough material available to show clearly

Fig. 3.3. Ploughman with his horse followed by a sower broadcasting seed corn, eighteenth century. The Library of the European Tradition.

that each branch of agriculture had its own secrets and those were communicated in the form of an admission into the craft" (Newman 1940, 36–37). As with many rural fraternities and urban guilds, there was an initiation ceremony for first-timers trading at the Sturbridge Fair. Initiations took place at one of the temporary hostelries, the Robin Hood, on the evening of the Horse Fair. It is clear that not everything of the initiation is recorded in the account published in 1828 in *The Mirror of Literature, Amusement and Instruction*. The initiation is dated to the 1760s. What is known is that the postulant was seated in an armchair with his head uncovered and his shoes off. In the room were his sponsors, the oddfathers, and a verger bearing a stave and a candle stood on either side of the postulant's chair. The officiator, clad in an academic cap and gown and holding a handbell, recited the following:

> *Over thy head I ring this bell*
> *Because thou art an infidel.*
> *And I know thee by thy smell.*

With a hoccius proxius mandamus
Let no vengeance light upon him
And so call upon him.

This child was born in the Merry Month of May
Clap a pound of butter to his cheek and it will melt
          away
And if he longs for a sup, let him have it, I may
From his hoccius proxius mandamus
Let no vengeance light upon him
And so call upon him.

This child's shoes are made from running leather
He'll run from father and mother the Deuce knows
          whither
And here he may turn the length of his tether
To a hoccius proxius mandamus
Let no vengeance light upon him
And so call upon him.

This child now to Sturbridge Fair is come
He may kiss a pretty wench ere he returns home
But let him be advised and not to Barnwell roam
For a hoccius proxius mandamus
Let no vengeance light upon him
And so call upon him.

Who names this child? [Sponsor gives a name. e.g.
          Nimble Heels, Stupid Stephen, Tommy Simper . . .]
Nimble Heels henceforward shall be his name
Which to confess let him not feel shame
Whether 'fore Master, Miss or Dame
With a hoccius proxius mandamus

Let no vengeance light upon him
And so call upon him.

This child first having paid his dues
Is welcome now to put on his shoes
And sing a song or tell a merry tale he may choose
About a hoccius proxius mandamus
Let no vengeance light upon him
And so call upon him.

Then hand the can unto our jolly Friar
And laugh and sing to our own hearts' desire
And when our wine is out, let all to bed retire
With a hoccius proxius mandamus
Let no vengeance light upon him
And so call upon him.

Sturbridge Fair ceased to be a trade mart in 1855 (Starsmore 1975, 11–12). River traffic was badly hit by the new railways, and Sturbridge Common, a convenient unloading point for goods from fen lighters plying the Cam, had no railway station or goods depot. As the town expanded in Victorian times, Sturbridge Common was surrounded by houses occupied by the working class, which deterred moneyed visitors from coming to what they saw as a dangerous place. The temporary streets of the fair had buildings built on the sites of the booths, and so in that part of the town today are Garlic Row, Oyster Row, and Mercer's Row, which exist on the lines of the fair's rows of booths.

The Oyster House, paradoxically on Garlic Row, which became a permanent building, continued as a public house until the 1950s. In the latter years of the Sturbridge Fair in the early twentieth century, this was a venue for the musicians in eastern Cambridge, south of the river. The upper floor of the Oyster House was a dance floor where local musicians played. The last to play there at fair time were Charlie

Huntlea (Anglia harp), Harry Day (whistles), and Herb Reynolds (concertina) (Wortley 1972). One of the favorite tunes played at the Oyster House was "We Won't Go Home Till Morning," of which only the second verse is commonly known as "For He's a Jolly Good Fellow." This was sung when the landlord said he was closing.

> *We won't go home till morning,*
> *We won't go home till morning,*
> *We won't go home till morning,*
> *And so say all of us.*
>
> *And so say all of us,*
> *And so say all of us,*
> *We won't go home till morning,*
> *We won't go home till morning,*
> *We won't go home till morning,*
> *And so say all of us.*

And when the landlord relented and, mock grudgingly, agreed to stay open or, after the introduction of licensing hours in World War I, declared a lock-in, the drinkers sang:

> *For he's a jolly good fellow,*
> *For he's a jolly good fellow,*
> *For he's a jolly good fellow,*
> *And so say all of us.*
> *And so say all of us,*
> *And so say all of us,*
> *For he's a jolly good fellow,*
> *For he's a jolly good fellow,*
> *For he's a jolly good fellow,*
> *And so say all of us.*

The Sturbridge Fair was held for the final time in 1933, being opened officially by the mayor of Cambridge, Florence Keynes. She noted that it was a curious ceremony that, because very few people were there, had lost all meaning except as a memento of past glories (Keynes 1950, 98–99). The fair was legally abolished by an order of the secretary of state in 1934. The derelict Oyster House was demolished in 1960 when the tanks, which once had kept thousands of oysters alive during the fair, were discovered under the building. They were destroyed. Relics of the town were considered unworthy of preservation. The last vestiges of the fair were suppressed in 1969 when rubble was dumped across the entrances to the common by order of the city council to keep out travelers who until then had continued to visit Stourbridge Common annually at fair time after the official discontinuance of the fair.

"HAVE YOU BEEN SWORN AT HIGHGATE?"— SWEARING ON THE HORNS

A number of similar initiations or challenges are recorded from stopping places along the great drovers' roads that ran toward London. At places where cattle fairs and markets were held, the drovers and traders in livestock held court at one of the inns. By means of recognition, any person who claimed to be a bona fide drover showed his skill by holding a bullock by the horns. A ritual appears to have developed from this into a symbolic and then speculative Swearing on the Horns, but a pair of horns was still used in the rite (Newman 1940, 36–37). At Highgate is the custom of Swearing on the Horns, which closely relates to the drovers' initiation, "taking the bull by the horns," but does not use a live animal.

> *It's a custom at Highgate*
> *That all who go through,*
> *Must be sworn on the horns, sir!*
> *And so, sir, must you!*

Bring the horns!—shut the door!
Now, sir, take off your hat!
When you come here again,
Don't forget to mind that!

In *The Gentleman's Magazine* in 1754, a writer commented that he had been much offended at the amazing quantity of horns always to be seen at Highgate, "some fixt on long Poles, some on Walking Staves, and some in the Inn rooms neatly gilt and decorated" (*Gentleman's Magazine* 1754, 16–17). The village of Highgate took its name from the gate across the road into London at that point, a stopping place for drovers and their herds. When it was observed and written about, early in the nineteenth century, the rite of Swearing on the Horns had become a ceremony to get money out of coach passengers who stopped at Highgate for refreshments "to the private advantage of public landlords." In the mid-eighteenth century, "upwards of eighty stages stopped every day at the Red Lion and that out of every five passengers three were sworn." Passengers were asked if they had been "sworn at Highgate," and if they replied "no," then the horns were brought in by the landlord. The person who had admitted noninitiation was then forced to undergo the ritual.

In 1826, a man called Guiver, the landlord of the Fox and Crown, was the officiant in the Swearing on the Horns ritual there. He was described as wearing a domino with a wig and mask. He held a book containing the oath. The staff with the horns was held by an old villager who acted as his clerk, and at every pause he called out "Amen!" The horns were attached to a pole about five feet in height. They were stood next to the person who was to be sworn. The candidate took off his or her hat, and when all there were bareheaded, the landlord then proclaimed, "Up standing and uncovered! Silence! Take notice what I now say unto you, for *that* is the first word of your oath— mind, *that!* You must acknowledge me to be your adopted father; I must acknowledge you to be my adopted son. If you do not call me father, you forfeit a bottle of wine; if I do not call you son, I forfeit the same. And now, my good son, if you are traveling through this village of Highgate and you have no money in your pocket, go call for a bottle of wine at any house you think it proper to go into, and book it to your father's score. If you have any friends with you, you may treat them as well, but if you have money of your own, you must pay for it yourself. For you must not say you have no money when you have, neither must you convey the money out of your own pocket into your friends' pockets, for I shall search you as well as them, and if it is found that you or they have money, you forfeit a bottle of wine for trying to cozen and cheat your poor old ancient father. You must not eat brown bread while you can get white, except that you like the brown the best; you must not drink small beer while you can get strong, except you like the small the best. You must not kiss the maid while you can kiss the mistress, except you like the maid the best, but sooner than lose a good chance you may kiss them both.

"And now, my good son, for a word or two of advice. Keep from all houses of ill repute, and every place of public resort for bad company. Beware of false friends, for they will turn to be your foes, and inveigle you into houses where you may lose your money and get no redress. Keep from thieves of every denomination. And now, my good son, I wish you a safe journey through Highgate and this life. I charge you, my good son, that if you know any in this company who have not taken this oath, you must cause them to take it, or make each of them forfeit a bottle of wine, for if you fail to do so you will forfeit a bottle of wine yourself. So now, my son, God bless you! Kiss the horns or a pretty girl if you see one here, which you like best, and so be free of Highgate!"

If a woman was in the room she was saluted, but if not, the horns had to be kissed. As soon as the salutation was over, the swearer-in commanded "Silence!" Then he said, "I have now to acquaint you with your privilege as a freeman of this place. If at any time you are going through Highgate and want to rest yourself and you see a pig lying in a ditch you have liberty to kick her out and take her place; but if you see three lying together you must only kick out the middle one and lie between the other two! God save the king! There is one circumstance essential for a freeman of Highgate to remember, and '*that* is the first word of his oath—mind *that!*' If he fail to recollect *that,* he is subject to be resworn from time to time, and so often, until he remember *that.* He is therefore never to forget the injunction before he swears, to take notice what is said, 'for *that* is the first word of your oath—mind *that,*' Failure of memory is deemed want of comprehension, which is no plea in the high court of Highgate—'mind *that!*' That is, that *that* 'that,' is '*that.*'"

At Highgate in the 1820s were nineteen inns or taverns that kept horns used in Swearing on the Horns. Every public house in Highgate had the horns at the door as a permanent sign. The Gate-House, the Crown, the Rose and Crown, the Angel, the Mitre, the Green Dragon, the Bull, the Bell and Horns, the Wrestlers, the Duke's Head, the Lord Nelson, and the Duke of Wellington all had stag's horns; the Coach and Horses, Castle, the Coopers' Arms, the Flask, the Fox and Crown, and the Red Lion, ram's horns; only the Red Lion and Sun had bullock's horns.

> *The Horn, the Horn,*
> *The lusty Horn,*
> *Is not a thing*
> *To mock or scorn.*

Along the drovers' roads in Hertfordshire "similar customs prevailed in other places as at Ware, and at the Griffin at Hoddesdon, etc." (Larwood and Hotten 1908, 108). In the early nineteenth century, the Griffin at Hoddesdon had the custom that "when any fresh waggoner came to that house with his team, a drinking horn, holding about a pint, fixed on a stand made of four rams' horns, was brought out of the house, and elevated above his head, and he was compelled to pay a gallon of beer, and to drink out of the horn" (Hone 1827).

The Horn Fair at Charlton in Kent, now part of South London, was held on Saint Luke's Day each year, attended by "the yearly collected rabble of mad-people at Horn Fair, the rudeness of which . . . may well be said to be insufferable." The New Year's Eve supper at the Swan Inn at Over the Cambridgeshire Fens included ceremonial drinking from a large cow horn called Long Tom or Long Tot (Porter 1969, 129–30). In North Devon was a custom that paraded horns in order to establish a cattle fair. It was a procession led by a man carrying a pair of ram's horns on a pole before a horse bearing two straw-filled effigies of a man and a woman riding back-to-back. They were followed by a noisy "tin-can band" of ladles, pots, frying pans, and the like, and the cracking of whips. At the end of the procession, the horns were nailed up (Bonser 1972, 235).

4

Secrets of the Trade and Craft Guilds

TRICKS OF THE TRADE

Every traditional trade and craft has its own legend of how it came into being, a story that contains a body of lore that preserves the secrets and tricks of the trade. Initiation of an apprentice into the fraternity involved elements from that trade's legendarium and was a ritual that impressed on the candidate the necessity not to divulge the secrets to anyone or even talk about them except to another sworn brother of the fraternity. There were standard questions and answers, passwords and words of recognition, rhymes, songs, physical postures, handshakes, and grips that only the initiates knew. Each craft and trade possessed a whole symbolic language unrecognizable to anyone outside the fraternity. Fragments of these symbolic shibboleths have passed into everyday speech, most particularly from Freemasonry, which, it must be emphasized, however, was only one of many similar secret orders practicing or derived from operative trades.

Many of the elements of initiation and recognition are common to more than one trade or craft. Other rites and ceremonies of clubs and secret societies also share many common features. Often, because Freemasonry is the best known and apparently most widespread of these orders, having survived the banning orders of 1797 and 1799 that drove the others underground, many writers assume that Masonic ritual is the origin of all other societies' ritual. This is especially true of writers who are Freemasons. But the sheer quantity and diversity of groups makes it more likely that the common features of the rites and ceremonies of the Freemasons and others have a common origin, not that all others are derivative from Freemasonry. Among the groups that use or used ritual, there are friendly societies, magical orders, craft guilds, trade unions, protest organizations, and political groups, usually clandestine and many of them dissident or revolutionary in intention. Many have existed in this country in the last four hundred years, of which little is known about them but their name.

Working people who had sought-after skills banded together in their own organizations that looked after their interests and prevented trade secrets from being used by nonmembers. Admission was through a ritual, usually in the form of a harrowing initiation. Formal groups that are known to have performed some initiatory rites of this kind include shoemakers, Horsemen, ploughboys, free farmers, free

Fig. 4.1. Fraternal or Masonic symbols on a doorhead, early nineteenth century, Sheffield.

gardeners, wild herb men, drovers, millers, brewers, colliers, free miners, charcoal burners, stonemasons, bricklayers, shearmen, horse traders, fair showmen, river boatmen, seamen, herring smokers, foresters, and Oddfellows. Their rites and ceremonies, as well as the secrets and tricks of the trade, were propagated orally by the members themselves, so that accurate records are few and in most cases absent. Initiates were compelled to swear a solemn and binding oath that bound them to disclose nothing, on pain of dire penalties resulting in their death. The Freemasons' death penalty was removed from the oath in 1986 (Hamill 1986, 59–60). Very few ever divulged the secrets that were entrusted to them; the secrets of the Horsemen were divulged and published, especially after the time when horses ceased to be used commonly in ploughing (see Singer 1881; McAldowie 1896; MacPherson 1929; Ord 1920; Evans 1971; Tebbutt; Neat 2002; etc.).

An act of Parliament of 1797 prohibited the taking of "unlawful oaths," that is, oaths just made illegal by the act. The Unlawful Societies Act of 1799 banned groups who administered such "unlawful oaths." The Unlawful Societies Act outlawed organizations that held closed

Fig. 4.2. Fraternal symbol of clasped hands. All rural fraternities had certain secret handshakes, known as "grips."

meetings and organizations that were structured with branches answerable to national committees. Membership was punishable with transportation to a colony for seven years. The only group excepted from this law was the Freemasons. Attempts to suppress the Oddfellows and the Orange Order under the act led to litigation, which resulted finally in these groups' legalization. The act was used by the authorities to suppress trade organizations of all kinds, including workers' unions. In Yorkshire in 1802, a member of a shearmen's group was prosecuted for swearing an oath "to be true to the shearmen, and to see that none of them are hurt, and not to divulge any of their secrets." And in London in 1804, the Master Boot and Shoe Makers Brought organization took legal action under the 1799 act against the Association of Journeymen Boot and Shoe Makers because the union had elected officials and was thus illegal.

The acts of Parliament that outlawed oath taking drove further underground those organizations who refused to disband. The Horsemen in particular continued their secret rites and ceremonies. The words of such rites were often magical in character (Newman 1940, 32), and terrible penalties were specified for oath breakers. When organized groups of workers appeared in public, they were usually disguised, as in

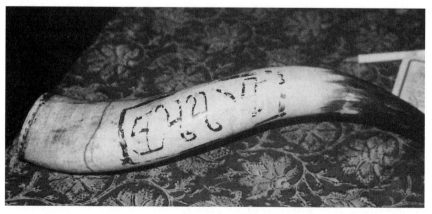

Fig. 4.3. A horn, probably from the early nineteenth century, inscribed with the name Baal in letters of the Theban alphabet. Discovered concealed in an old barn in Norfolk, it is likely to be an artifact once used in rituals of a rural fraternity, such as the Horsemen.

the Plough Monday traditions of the Confraternity of the Plough. From these clandestine activities came the commonly accepted code of unwritten rules, referred to as a charter in this part of England. The Fenman's Charter, for example, is the unwritten code of conduct of those who work in Fenland occupations. When disguised Northamptonshire and Cambridgeshire ploughboys and plough witches were remonstrated for driving ploughshares into the ground and destroying the gardens of those who would not give them money on Plough Monday, they replied, "There's no law in the world can touch us because it's an old charter."

THE CONFRATERNITY OF THE PLOUGH AND HORSEMANRY

Ploughmen who ploughed using horses as motive power were initiates of one or another of the Horsemen's fraternities. From pre-Roman times until the seventeenth century, "the labored ox" was used as a draft animal, especially in plough teams where its pulling power could cope with the heavy wooden ploughs in use before experiments were made to create a better plough. In the mid-seventeenth century, improvements to the plough appeared in the Netherlands, and farmers in Great Britain soon began to use these superior ploughs. In Rotherham, Yorkshire, a center of ironworking, the much lighter Rotherham swing plough was developed from the Dutch plough. Still constructed of timber, like the earlier ploughs, its coulter was made from iron and the moldboard and share were also reinforced with iron plates. The Rotherham plough rapidly superseded earlier ploughs because it required less traction to plough with it. This enabled horses to be used in place of oxen. Use of the Rotherham plough spread widely across Great Britain, being manufactured on a large scale. In Scotland in 1763, John Small experimented with various new moldboard shapes, applying scientific calculations to them. Small came up with an optimal plough that could turn the soil more effectively using even less tractive effort than the Rotherham plough. This Scots plough is the origin of all modern ploughs.

The Confraternity of the Plough included all men who worked with the plough, whether drawn by oxen or horses. Just as they shod horses with iron horseshoes, blacksmiths also shod oxen with cues for draft work. Oxen were cheaper to shoe than horses, and this may have delayed the changeover to horse ploughing in some places (De Henley 1890, 13). The Plough Monday teams called plough stots and plough bullocks or bullockers are from districts where ploughing with oxen continued well into the nineteenth and even the twentieth century. In this region, oxen were in use at Brigg in Lincolnshire in 1853, at North Ormesby, also in Lincolnshire in 1858, and at Helmdon in Northamptonshire as late as 1902. A farmer at Luton in Bedfordshire used oxen until 1909 (Johnson 1912, 453). In Cambridgeshire, horses took over ploughing much earlier. Members of the Confraternity of the Plough, whether they worked with oxen or horses, had specialist knowledge about how to take care of animals and to train them to perform the necessary tasks expected of them. This information was acquired through apprenticeship as a ploughboy from the age of fourteen to twenty-one. At twenty-one, the ploughboy was initiated as a full member of the fraternity and was then fit to receive the secret teachings of the craft.

During the nineteenth century, several editions of a book by William Singer titled *An Exposition of the Miller and Horseman's Word, or the True System of Raising the Devil* were published in Aberdeen. Singer's text claimed to reveal details of the initiated secrets of the millers' and Horsemen's organizations. Both organizations had a "word" that was said to enable the user to perform seemingly miraculous feats. Noninitiates who are interested in such things frequently speculate whether the Horseman's undoubted powers come primarily from the intrinsic magical power of the Horseman's Word, from secret techniques taught only to initiates, from the inherent power of a frog or toad bone, or from the devil. But it must be noted that not all, but perhaps most, Horsemen were toadmen (see "The Toadmen and Toadwomen," page 67). This confusion is doubtless fostered by everyone who actually has the power (e.g., Singer 1881, 23; McAldowie 1896, 311; *Society of the Horseman's*

Grip and Word 2009). It is better to confuse people who need not know, rather than to divulge information needlessly, thereby breaking one's oaths. Magical texts like Singer's book must have fed into the wider rituals, procedures, and teachings within other secret groups operating in the countryside. Human culture is always in a state of change, never standing still as time passes, so the rituals of one year may be modified by the next one when new information is available to those who actually preside over the rites and ceremonies.

There appear to be three different schools or orders of country Horsemanry in Britain. They are not mutually exclusive to one another because they have overlapping elements and perhaps even membership. Because Horsemanry has never had an overall authority like the Free Gardeners or the Oddfellows, it is known by different names in different parts of eastern England. In Huntingdonshire, it is called the Horseman's Guild (Tebbutt 1984, 85), and farther south and east, the Society of the Horseman's Word (Evans 1971, 227–39). The Society of the Horseman's Word, best documented in Scotland, where it is believed to have originated when ploughing with horses was introduced there in the eighteenth century, is also operative in East Anglia. The Society of the Horseman's Word is subdivided into two divisions or lineages, called Marshall and Johnston.

As well as the Society of the Horseman's Word, in eastern England there are those who practice the Whisper* and those who are toadmen. Leslie Newman claimed in 1940 that Scottish workers had brought the Society of the Horseman's Word from Scotland to eastern England in the second half of the nineteenth century (Newman 1940, 38). But perhaps it arrived earlier, when the Scots plough was introduced to this part of England in the eighteenth century and men who knew how to use it came with it to teach ploughmen who hitherto had worked with oxen. George Ewart Evans refers to the hereditary transmission of Horsemanry in East Anglia, acknowledging the Scots element there but denying it a Scottish origin: "We had it before the Scots came down. My father was

---

*The Whisper is associated with Gypsies and farriers who are not in the Horsemen's society.

born in 1862: he had it and my grandfather had it before him" (Evans 1961, 272). But whether by this he meant the Whisper or the Horseman's Word is unclear. It appears that toadmen were not unknown in Scotland either, and blacksmiths were eligible for membership in the Society of the Horseman's Word (MacPherson 1929, 290; Ord 1920).

The Society of the Horseman's Word is the best known of these groups, perhaps because it was publicized in several books by Evans in the late 1950s and early 1960s. There was a privately owned manuscript notebook written in Girton, near Cambridge, with what looked like nineteenth-century handwriting. I was allowed to look through it in the early 1970s, but not to copy it, and it appeared to be a catechism of Horsemanry. I do not know what happened to it. The initiation in Scotland and East Anglia involves a series of physical and mental ordeals, literally harrowing experiences that culminate in the initiate being forced to swear the Horseman's Oath (Evans 1971, 230–31). And even after that, further ordeals can be expected. In its form of words, this oath includes dreadful penalties for breaking it, and the initiates experience what they mean at first hand.

The actual Horseman's Word used by different groups varies, for the fraternities are decentralized with no overall authority, transmission of knowledge being strictly local, from man to man. One version of the Horseman's Whisper current in Cambridgeshire is the Latin *sic jubeo* (thus I command) (Porter 1958, 116; Bayliss 1997, 12); others from the Society of the Horseman's Word divulged in Scotland are "One" (Singer 1881, 23) and "Both in One," which is imparted over "a grip o' the Auld Chiel's hand" (the devil's hand), which actually was a stick covered with a hairy skin or a cow's foot with its cloven hoof covered with a luminous substance to make it glow in the dark and terrify the initiate (MacPherson 1929, 291; Singer 1881, 8). Thus, "the Horseman's Grip and Word" refers both to taking the devil's hand in the initiation and the secret handshakes by which initiates who are members can recognize one another. Not only Freemasons have secret handshakes and signs of recognition.

The second group of Horsemen in eastern England who have the power are those with the Whisper, which was well established in Hertfordshire and Cambridgeshire. Leslie Newman, writing in 1940, tells us that men operating with the Whisper are not members of the Society of the Horseman's Word, but part of "another, and indigenous fraternity that frankly employs magical cures." Unlike the Horseman's Word, this tradition was not brought from Scotland, but seems to have been spread in eastern England by Romani travelers (Newman 1940, 39). It was known to great effect in eighteenth-century Ireland, where it was also said to have a Romani origin.

The word used in the Whisper in Cambridgeshire was divulged at the beginning of the twentieth century by Ephraim Smith of Hilgay Fen, who, on his deathbed, impoverished in the Downham Market

Fig. 4.4. Great Gransden windmill, drawing by the author.

Workhouse, passed it on—*sic jubeo* (thus I command) (Porter 1958, 116). Ephraim Smith was a man "of gypsy stock" who said he had received it through ancestral transmission. Newman observed that these secrets were claimed in the past by many country people and probably were spread originally by the Romani Gypsies. But the "close corporation of Gypsies" as unofficial veterinarians has been "broken up by police action, by legislation, and the development of modern veterinary science" (Newman 1940, 39).

THE MIRACLE OF BREAD

According to one Horsemen's catechism from Cambridgeshire and Suffolk, "The Word was imprisoned between black boards and chained and padlocked in the pulpit of the church. It was impossible for it to get free among the plough and the nets, that the season of famine be at an end; therefore, the lesser world of the fiddle, the rune, the word spoken, must work the miracle of bread." This Miracle of Bread links the society of Horsemen with the millers, another group in possession of the Word. The ploughmen prepare the ground, sow, and harrow in the grain. It grows, is harvested by the laborers, transported, and threshed and then taken to the mill, where the miller grinds the grain into flour. The Miracle of Bread has six stations or stages.

The Plough
The Seed
The Green Corn
The Yellow Corn
The Stones
Rising Again

The first magical act of the Miracle of Bread is the ploughing of the field, forming straight rigs (furrows) on the field in which to sow the grain. The rite of "setting the rig" uses two willow sticks, each called

Fig. 4.5. A wheat sheaf pattern stamped in plaster on the outside of a house in Saffron Walden, Essex, in the technique known as pargetting.

a dod, which are set up at each end of the furlong to be ploughed and both activated magically and made visible by wisps of straw tied near the top. The ploughman lines up his horses in front of one dod and looks toward the other dod at the end of the furlong, noting what is visible behind it, a back-mark called "the farthest beacon." The first furrow is drawn straight toward the second dod, keeping the farthest beacon in sight. The rest of the furrows are ploughed parallel with the first one.

The Miracle of Bread centers on the cycle of the growing grain, rather as the traditional English ballad "John Barleycorn Must Die" tells of the emergence of the barley plant from the seemingly dead grain buried in the earth and its seasonal development in time until the cycle is completed and begins anew. In the larger, more organized lodges were degrees based on various progressive states of the growing grain, as in the song.

But the primary function of any system is to be effective, and like other handicraft skills, Horsemanry is an art tried and tested in the harsh world of physical reality. If it did not work, it would soon have faded into oblivion.

The third current of Horsemanry is part of toadmanry. It is said that those who possess the power of the Horseman's Word can stop a man in his tracks, can stop a plough team, can make a plough plough a rig without a man or horse, and can make a horse come to the possessor of the Word (Davidson 1956, 68–69). The newly initiated Horseman is given the Word "between the collar and the hames." The collar is

Fig. 4.6. Traditional forms of bread, including the human form. Tenby, Wales.

a cushion made of leather that is stuffed with straw and fitted round the horse's neck. The hames are the metal rods curved to fit the collar and fixed to it. The traces of the shafts are secured to the hames, which grip the collar very closely. The expression "between the collar and the hames" therefore means that there should be complete integration of action between man and horse during the work. A Scottish catechism tells that the first horse collar was made with Tubal Cain's trousers stuffed with *saigs* (iris plants) (*Society of the Horseman's Grip and Word* 2009, 110).

Of course, as with all secret knowledge, the techniques of Horsemanry could not be kept totally secret, being known also by others who were not directly connected with organized transmission of the techniques. Eventually, they were published. But despite the techniques' appearance in the public domain, one still cannot be a member of a practical fraternity without joining it. And to join it, one must be initiated.

5

Secrets of the Horsemen

THE HORSEMAN'S INITIATION

The initiation of a man into the Society of the Horseman's Grip and Word has been described by a number of authors who have received the information from oath breakers. First, the candidate for initiation is summoned. A horsehair in an envelope is one means. He is instructed to go to a particular place where he will be met. But nothing is what it seems. In one version, the candidate was told to go to a graveyard on a particular night and look near a particular tombstone, where he would find a whip that would give him power over horses. When he arrived at the grave, he would be grabbed by men waiting for him and taken to the barn where the initiation was to be conducted (Evans 1965, 222). In the ballad "John Barleycorn Must Die," after they cut him down and bound him to the cart,

> They wheeled him round and round the field
> Till they came upon a barn,
> And there they swore a solemn vow
> On old John Barleycorn.

The candidate is bound and blindfolded and disorientated by being taken by crooks and straits, devious pathways called the Crooked Path,

to ... ce w... ...will be initiated. This crooked path symbolizes
th... ...ltie ...of li... but even though he is disorientated, he has noth-
in... fear b... ...use his would-be brothers are guiding him to the right
pla... It also symbolizes the early training of the young horse because
the candidate for initiation is equally an untrained "colt." Eventually, he
arrives at the destination. Here, in the barn, the bound candidate must
submit to the ordeals, the harrowing experiences that will make him a
member of Horsemanry.

After being manhandled around the four corners of the barn and
offered a drink of what appears to be horse urine, the candidate is
brought to the center of the "Horseman's hall"; his blindfold is removed
and he finds himself standing before a man impersonating a dangerous
entity, identified variously as the devil, Lucifer, Auld Clootie, Old Nick,
Hercules, and so on (*Society of the Horseman's Grip and Word* 2009, 88).

Fig. 5.1. Horseman, the late Tony Harvey, at Gressenhall, Norfolk, 1995. He
is wearing a traditional Horseman's suit, with a "full brace" of
buttons in threes. Each button, made of horn, has the
emblem of the seven-holed horseshoe on it.

Here he is asked questions, being prompted to m███ ████rrect answers, which may begin with something like:

> OFFICIANT: "How came you hither?"
> CANDIDATE: "Through darkness, dangers and difficulties."
> OFFICIANT: "What do you seek to obtain?"
> CANDIDATE: "The lost Word," and so on.

After this symbolic question-and-answer session, whose form of words is reminiscent of some mummers' plays, the candidate is made to take the Horseman's Oath. It must be taken in a position "neither sitting, walking nor swinging, lying, flying, standing clothed nor unclothed, boots on or boots off or blind" (*Society of the Horseman's Grip and Word* 2009, 89). Here is a Cambridgeshire version of the Horseman's Oath, dating from the early twentieth century.

> I of my own free will and accord do solemnly vow and swear before God that I will always hele, [variant of heal] conceal and never reveal any art or part of this secret of horsemanry which is to be revealed to me at this time, or any other time hereafter, except to a true and faithful brother after finding him so after due trial and strict examination. Furthermore I vow and I swear I will not give it or see it given to a fool nor to a madman nor to a drunkard nor to anyone in drink nor to anyone who would abuse or badly use his own or his master's horses.
>
> Furthermore I vow and I swear that I will not give it nor see it given to a tradesman excepting to a blacksmith or a farrier or to a worker of horses. Furthermore I vow and I swear that I will not give it or see it given to anyone under eighteen or above forty-five years of age nor without the sum of one pound sterling or anything of the same value being placed upon the table as I do at this time before three lawful sworn brethren after trial and examination finding them to be so.
>
> Furthermore I vow and I swear that I will not give it nor see

it given to anyone after the sun sets on Saturday night nor before she rises on Monday morning nor in a public house. Furthermore I vow and I swear that I will always be at a brother's call within the bounds of three miles except I can give lawful excuse such as my wife in childbed or my mares in foaling or myself in bad health or my master's employment. Furthermore I vow and I swear that I will not give it to my father nor mother, sister nor brother, nor to a woman at all.

Furthermore I vow and I swear that I will not write it nor indict it, paint nor print it, carve nor engrave it, in the valleys or on the hill-side, on rock nor gravel, sand nor snow, silver nor gold, brass nor copper, iron nor steel, woollen nor silk, nor anything moveable or immovable under the great canopy of heaven. Or so much wave a single letter of it in the air whereby the secrets of horsemanry might be revealed.

And if I fail in any of these obligations that I go under at this time or at any time hereafter, I ask to my heart's wish and desire that my throat may be cut from ear to ear with a horseman's knife, my body torn to pieces between two wild horses and blown by the four winds of heaven to the uttermost parts of the earth, my heart torn from my left breast and its blood wrung out and buried in the sands of the seashore where the tide ebbs and flows thrice every night and day that my remembrance may be no longer held among true and faithful brethren, so help me God to keep this solemn obligation. (Sid Smith, personal communication; cf. variant from A. A. Dent, quoted in Evans 1966, 230–31; *Society of the Horseman's Grip and Word* 2009, 89–91)

A published version of the oath from Scotland makes the distance one must go to help a brother in distress five miles, rather than three (*Society of the Horseman's Grip and Word* 2009, 90). After the oath, the sworn brother is tested. The test is a trick, and, of course, he fails it. Then he is arraigned as an oath breaker and sentenced to hang. He is taken to the hayloft, shown a noose attached to a roof beam, blind-folded again, and a noose is put around his neck. Then he is pushed off the beam and falls. But the noose is not the same one he was shown. It is not attached to the beam, and he falls onto a pile of hay, which breaks his fall. Then the devil-man takes off the blindfold and welcomes him as a true and sworn Horseman. After that, he is given a lecture that describes the mythical origin of Horsemanry, the rules of Horsemanry, the Horseman's Word, and the signs of recognition.

BELL AND STAR

According to the Horsemans' Society legendarium, taught at the time of initiation, Bell and Star were the names of the first mare and stallion because there was a star on his brow and a bell on her brow (*Society of the Horseman's Grip and Word* 2009, 111). The bell is allied with the star as both are symbols of guidance. The lead horse's bell guides

Fig. 5.2. Carters Sydney and Edward Dale, the author's great-uncles, on a horse-drawn cart in Chartham, Kent, 1914. Sidney Dale was killed two years later in the Battle of the Somme, aged twenty-two. From the Pennick Family Archives.

the packhorse train, while the leading star whose place always remains the same in the sky permits navigation at sea and on land. This is the Pole Star, called Polaris or the Nowl, the nail around which the heavens rotate like the hub of a wheel. The *stella non erratica* (the unerring star) has a medieval Latin motto for its emblem, *qui me non aspicet errat* (he who does not look at me goes astray). Two stars of the constellation of the Plough point to the Nowl; the seven nails in the horseshoe symbolize the seven stars of the Plough (Tony Harvey, personal communication). In their work on inn signs, Larwood and Hotten state:

> The Bell and Horse is an old and still frequent sign; it occurs on trades tokens; as John Harcourt at the Bell and Black Horse in Finsbury, 1668, and on various others; whilst at the present day it may be seen at many a roadside alehouse. Bells were a favourite feature of horse trappings in the middle ages. Geoffrey Chaucer's abbot is described:
>
> > *When he rode men his bridle hear,*
> > *Gingling in a whistling wind as clere,*
> > *And eke as loud as doth a chapel bell.*
> > (LARWOOD AND HOTTEN 1908, 113)

Leland's *Collectanea* contains the text of a manuscript from the Cottonian Library (Leland 1770, 279, H7) that records the journey of Margaret of England to Scotland, there to be married to King James. There are numerous mentions of these bells in this text. The horse of Sir William Harguil, companion of Sir William Conyers, sheriff of Yorkshire, is described as "his Hors Harnays full of campanes [bells] of silver and gylt." The master of the horse of the Duke of Northumberland was "monted apon a gentyll horse, and campanes of silver and gylt," and a company of knights, "some of their hors harnes was full of campanes, sum of gold and sylver, and others of gold" (Leland 1770).

It was the custom in medieval times to give a golden bell as the reward of a race. In Chester, such a bell was run for yearly on

Saint George's day; it was "dedicated to the kinge, being double gilt with the Kynges Armes upon it, and was carried in the procession by a man on horseback upon a septer in pompe, and before him a noise of trumpets in pompe." This custom of racing for a bell led to the adoption of the phrase, still common in the nineteenth century, "bearing off the bell" (Larwood and Hotten 1908, 174–75). And the Horseman's song, sung in the "magical" key E minor, goes:

> *Of all the horses in the merry green wood*
> *The bob-tail mare bears the bell away.*
> (JOHN THORNE, PERSONAL COMMUNICATION)

The ballad "Thomas of Ersseldoune" tells of the encounter between the bard Thomas and the queen of Elfland. Bells were part of the harness of her dapple-gray palfrey.

> *Hir payetrelle was of iralle fyne;*
> *Hir cropoure was of orfare;*
> *And als clere golde hir brydill it schone;*
> *One aythir syde hange bellys three.*
> (CHILD 1860, 97–108)

Similarly, the queen of Fairyland's horse is bedecked with bells in the ballad "Sir John Gordon," collected by John Ord in his *Bothy Songs and Ballads*. Sir John encounters the queen of Faerie and is taken away

Fig. 5.3. Bell in leaded glass, early twentieth century. The Bell Inn, Nottingham.

to the Otherworld, where he serves her. Of the queen of Fairyland, the ballad says:

> *Her gown was o' the green, green silk,*
> *Her mantle o' velvet fine,*
> *And from the mane of her milk-white steed*
> *Silver bells hung fifty and nine.*

(ORD [1930] 1995, 423)

THE TOADMEN AND TOADWOMEN

Many horsemen carry these bones with them still.

(BALES 1939, 69)

The use of the toad bone is closely connected with the Horseman's Guild, because the power to control horses can be gained by becoming a toadman. According to oral lore, it involves the would-be toadman performing a certain ritual to select the witch-bone, after which the postulant had to be accepted by the devil. It was reputed to be "a ritual no decent man would undergo" (Rudkin 1936, 24). According to Enid Porter, the person possessing this power was known as a toadman "because to qualify as such he had to carry out a secret rite involving a pact with the Devil" (Porter 1969, 55). The toad-bone ritual is universally recognized as the means of gaining supernatural power over horses. Knowledge of it has circulated in the public domain for a long time. It appeared in the first half of the nineteenth century in a book of horse doctors' techniques, *The Country Horse-Doctor,* published at Swaffham in Norfolk in 1835. "To make a horse lay down," it says, "get some grey toads, hang them on a white-thorn bush until they are dead, then lay them in an ant-hill . . . put them into a stream . . . dry them and beat them to a powder, touch a Horse on the shoulder to jade him and on the rump to draw him" (Chumbley 2001). J. W. Saville repeated the recipe verbatim in his *The Horse-Keeper's Receipt Book* in 1878. Of

Fig. 5.4. A toad bone.

a person who has conducted this ritual, it is said that "he has been to the river."

The Norfolk witch Tilley Baldrey had her techniques published in the *Eastern Counties Magazine* in 1901. She tells how she became a witch through the toad-bone ritual. In standard English: "You catch a hopping toad and carry it in your bosom until it has rotted away to the back-bone, then you take it and hold it over running water at midnight till the Devil comes to you and pulls you over the water." This is the initiation as a witch. Baldrey has many tales attached to her, including a successful death-curse placed on her husband's lover. In West Norfolk, this magic bone is called the witch-bone (Bales 1939, 69). Some statements by self-confessed toadmen and toadwomen explicitly speak of the devil in connection with the toad-bone ritual, for "a toadman was accounted a kind of witch" (Evans 1961, 246). However, Huntingdonshire folklorist C. F. Tebbutt characterized it as "one form of witchcraft with no menace to others" (Tebbutt 1984, 85). Enid Porter recounted a report from 1949 from a man at March that the toadman had to carry the bone to the stables at midnight on three consecutive nights for the final initiation (Porter 1969, 56). The inference is, from other accounts, that the final ritual of admission would take place there.

Another element of the rite was described by the Norfolk Horseman Albert Love. He called the rite the Water of the Moon and specifies that the ritual be performed at the full moon (Evans 1965, 217–18). In 1915, Catherine Parsons described the toad-bone ritual as practiced in southern Cambridgeshire: "At Horseheath it is believed that, if an ordinary toad be put into a tin pierced with holes and buried in an ant-hill until the ants have devoured all the toad's flesh, and the bones be taken out of the tin at twelve o'clock at night and thrown into a running stream, the bones which float up the stream can be used for witching purposes" (Parsons 1915, 37).

For hundreds of years, Newmarket in Cambridgeshire has been a center of horse racing, and lore and techniques of the grooms there includes the bone ritual, using a frog: "Grooms catch a frog and keep it in a bottle or tin until nothing but the bones remain. At New Moon they draw these upstream in running water; one of the bones which floats is kept as a charm in the pocket or hung round the neck. This gives the man the power to control any horse, however vicious it may be" (Burn 1914, 363–64). At Bourn in Cambridgeshire, George Kirk worked as a blacksmith. He possessed a frog's bone that gave him power over horses. One of his helpers who worked with him in 1908 gave an account of his powers. Kirk was known for his remarkable control of horses at the forge, and the helper naturally asked him how it was done. Kirk told him to take a frog and put it in an anthill and put the bones in a stream, where the bone would reveal itself. "Keep this bone, and you can then give yourself to the devil and have the power I have got." Kirk, however, warned his helper not to do it. "Take my advice and don't; you will never rest if you do" (Tebbutt 1984, 85).

George Ewart Evans tells about a stallion leader who had the frog's bone who got a terrible fright when he had a horse come to his bedside at night. His wife also told him that nothing would bake properly in the house. He felt he was going crazy because of the frog's bone and decided to get rid of it. So he dug a deep hole, put the bone in a tin filled with milk and vinegar, and buried it. He was no longer worried, but equally he could no longer get on well with his horses (Evans 1965, 238). The doom that descends on toadmen and toadwomen is well known. They are driven by the power and react by entering "the house of darkness," falling prey to melancholy and depression. Many commit suicide, if before that they are not overcome at night by the Black Ghost, which leaves one gasping for breath, or dead.

The man known as Himself or the King of the Norfolk Poachers also wrote about the toad-bone ritual. He put the toad in a perforated box and buried it in a nest of black ants. Once the ants had eaten away the flesh, the toad was exhumed and taken at midnight on Saint Mark's Eve to a running stream and thrown into the water. The bone that swam upstream was taken out, and then the devil granted the power of witchcraft, which one can use to control men and animals, a necessary ability for a professional poacher ("King of the Norfolk Poachers" 1935, 13–14).

Possessing the power of the bone gives the toadman control over not only horses but also cattle, pigs, and women, and the toadwoman control over horses, cattle, pigs, and men (John Thorne, personal com-

Fig. 5.5. Toad bone in locket. Cambridgeshire, nineteenth century.

munication). The toad or frog bone bestows on the initiate the ability to see in the dark, to become invisible, and to steal without getting caught. Toadmen were feared and admired for their extraordinary powers. "No door is ever closed to a toadman" is said in the Fens (Pattinson 1953, 425). The Fenland farmworker Arthur Randall wrote in his memoirs, *Sixty Years a Fenman,* of a toadman he worked with in 1911. This man was a head Horseman who was always said to be able to make locked doors fly open by throwing his cap at them (Randall 1966, 110–11).

A recipe for stealing extra corn to feed one's horses was recorded in 1933 from a wagoner at Digby in Lincolnshire. It involved catching a frog, killing it, and taking out its heart. The frog was then buried and the wagoner carried the heart, which gave the wagoner the ability to pass through the small holes cut in barn doors that allow the cats to come and go. In this way, he could take the extra corn (Rudkin 1933, 289). Of another farmworker after World War II it was said, "Pig feed rationing in the war meant nothing to him: he was a toadman" (Pattinson 1953, 425). A story is told from 1930 when a Norfolk man stood a walking stick against a wall and then beckoned it to come toward him, which it did. The shaken witness later learned that the owner of the stick was a toadman who had "one of these bones" (Bales 1939, 70). A Horseman's walking stick is a useful tool, for it has an almost invisible cut in it just above the ferrule, where oils and other substances can be secreted (Evans 1971, 210). It also has other magical functions, as Bales's account shows.

There is an East Anglian dialect word, *tudding,* referring to being bewitched or cursed—"putting the toad" on someone. The Cambridgeshire Fenman W. H. Barrett wrote in *More Tales from the Fens* a story that tells of Crazy Moll, a horse-stopping witch who affected an animal so that people encountering it said, "That animal's tudded." In another story set on Hallowe'en, he and his comrades encounter witches and are afraid that "some of us will be tudded before morning" (Barrett and Porter 1964, 121, 135). A person who had been bewitched says that someone has "put the toad on him" (Bales 1939, 66–75), and in 1929 the Norfolk folklorist Mark Taylor recounted how "an old lady of E— whom I annoyed 'set a toad on me' about four years ago" (Taylor 1929, 126–27). East Anglians who are known by the nickname Tuddy are always treated with respect.

URBAN HORSES

During the Industrial Revolution, as society became more urbanized, horses were still initially used for transport. Large numbers of horses were needed for both goods and passenger transport in cities. The Society of the Horseman's Word and the Whisperers taught their initiates that they should look after their horses well and never mistreat them. A Scottish convivial toast used by members of the Horseman's Society tells us:

> *Here's to them that can work horses,*
> *Bad luck to them that is cruel,*
> *Let perseverance be their guide,*
> *And nature be their rule.*
> (SOCIETY OF THE HORSEMAN'S GRIP
> AND WORD 2009, 120)

The nineteenth-century Scottish bothy ballad "Nicky Tams"* (the Scots word for lalligags) is about a Horseman initiated into the Society of the Horseman's Grip and Word who considers leaving working on the land to gain employment on the horse trams (streetcars) or join the mounted police (Ord [1939] 1995, 18). But it is clear that most of the men who worked with horses in the urban setting were not initiated Horsemen. Horses used by the railway companies for transporting merchandise to and from rail goods depots were generally kept in good condition. But some transport operations, clearly not manned

---

*Farmworkers used to tie string or laces around the knees of their trousers. In Scotland these ties were called "nicky tams" and in East Anglia "lalligags."

by Horsemanry initiates, did not treat their animals at all well. There are extant records of horsekeeping by large transport undertakings in nineteenth-century England, one of which is the *Horse Register* of the Derby Tramways Company. This was kept from 1880 until June 1907, when electric trams replaced the horse-drawn ones. On the Derby trams, horses worked as much as four hours a day, pulling the tramcar perhaps fifteen miles in that work period.

During a single working day on the Derby horse tram system, each tramcar would be pulled by four separate pairs of horses. In Cambridge a single horse was used to pull even a double-decker tramcar, ostensibly because the tramways had no gradients. Throughout the operation of horse trams in Cambridge—between 1880 to 1914, when the trams were replaced by motor buses—the press was filled with letters of complaint about the ill treatment of the tram horses. But writing to the press changed nothing. The Derby *Horse Register* gives the name, registration number, age on purchase, and the final fate of each horse or mare; the register contains many that were "worn out," that is, collapsed. There were considerable numbers of fatal injuries to tram horses: broken backs, ribs fractured, burst blood vessels, and heart attacks, clearly symptoms of overwork. No initiated member of the Society of the Horseman's Grip and Word would ever have treated horses in such an unkind manner.

6

Millers, Gardeners, and Bonesmen

THE MILLERS

Flour milling is a trade, which, like that of the Horsemen and the brewers, possesses a special password, which is also ascribed magical powers. Like the members of the Confraternity of the Plough, millers play their part in bringing about the Miracle of Bread. The Miller's Word is not as well documented as the Horseman's, for millers were always far smaller numerically than Horsemen. The Miller's Word was a society of grain millers whose function was to transmit the secret knowledge of the millers. As with other craft mysteries, it has an initiation that permits entry into the secrets of milling. As with the Horsemen and toadmen, the devil appears in the Miller's initiation. The actual Word, at least as used in Scotland, was published by William Singer and revealed as *Art*. Powers associated with the Miller's Word appear to have been less well regulated than the Horsemen's. As with the Horseman's Word, the Millers' is often taken literally as an incantation, a word of power that produces a magical effect directly.

But at a practical level, possession of the Word means knowing the mysteries of the craft. This gives one the ability to achieve the objectives of the trade through skills not known by noninitiates. It also confers nonmilling powers. Thus, the Miller's Word is said to give a Miller the power to stop or start a mill at will without touching it as well to stop horses, influence women, and gain invisibility (Singer 1881, 11; McAldowie 1896, 309–14). It also allows for serious misuse (Singer 1881, 10–11); in 1920, Glasgow Police Superintendent John Ord (who was an initiated Horseman) wrote that the Millers "taught their members nothing but evil." Possessors of the Miller's Word were reputed to have powers to produce telekinetic phenomena. Ord wrote, "Members of the 'Millers' society claimed the power to raise and stop such proceedings at will," but so far as he could learn, "there was nothing in their senseless tricks that could be attributed to the supernatural" (Ord 1920).

Members of the Miller's Word practiced a form of magic indistinguishable from common witchcraft. Even the techniques were the same. For example, a magical recipe given by William Singer from the Millers' magical repertoire is a spell "to make a girl tell you her mind." Its *materia magica* is the tongue of a frog that must be cut from the frog's mouth with an edge tool not made by hands, such as a piece of broken bottle. The frog must then make three leaps once its tongue is cut out or the spell loses the virtue. Then the frog's tongue must be pressed to the breast of the girl, or in her hand, "and she will tell you everything you wish to know" (Singer 1881, 13).

In this region, a story about the post-mill at Great Gransden in Huntingdonshire hints at the magical powers of millers. This windmill is now a scheduled ancient monument that stands isolated and unusable. Around 1930, Richard Webb recounted a story about his grandfather, William Webb, who was the last miller who worked the Great Gransden windmill. A brother of William's wife, who appears to have been a waster (a person who is work-shy and lives off the efforts of others) came to live at the mill house and died there. Among his belongings, his sister found a book. Richard Webb called this book his "infidel's bible." From its description, it appears to have been a "black book" or grimoire. The woman was too frightened even to touch it, but she used a pair of tongs to take it to the fire to burn it. But William saw what she was doing and told her to leave it, as he could make some money from it by selling it next time he went to town. Then he took the book from her. But he did not sell it, but instead hid it somewhere in the mill.

Then the mill stopped running, and he could no longer grind grain. Millwrights he called in to discover what had gone wrong and repair the fault could find nothing the matter with the structure or the machinery. As they could not fix the mill and it would not go, William had to dismiss his workers and give up milling. Three years after the business collapsed, Richard Webb came to live at the mill house. Then he found out about the "infidel's bible." He searched the mill and found it, brought it back to the house, and then his grandmother threw it into the fire, where it was destroyed. Then they set up the mill to run again, and it worked. The mill's failure to work was blamed on the presence of the black book.

In this tale, it was the presence of this "black book" that stopped

Fig. 6.1. Great Gransden windmill, now preserved but out of use.

the mill from working, but the arrival of someone who knew how to deal with the problem got the mill going again. Whether Richard Webb had the Miller's Word is not known. It was he who told the tale, and he was not likely to divulge membership to noninitiates. In any case, the mill did not work for much longer. It was last used in 1913 and today it is preserved as a picturesque relic (Tebbutt 1984, 83). Milling was a family trade, and elsewhere in Huntingdonshire the Watts family operated several mills. The last Huntingdonshire miller, who died in 1933, was Erastus Watts, who worked Hemingford Mill (Newell 1991, 58). So, like in some currents and lineages of Horsemanry and toadmanry, and certainly among the free farmers, the Miller's Word may have also been passed down in families from father to son.

Most windmills were named after their village, their builder, or their owner. But in eastern England, the custom of naming mills in the manner of those in the Netherlands was common. Even the smaller wind pumps and wind engines used for drainage in the Fens were named, the name often reflecting some perceived character of the place or the building. Along the Hundred Foot River were wind pumps called Baby, Black Bess, Granny, Granddad, Saucy Sally, and Hooded Maria, and Tilly, Goose, and Duck worked on the River Lark near Prickwillow, while between Brandon Creek and Littleport were Ape's Face, Bandy, Bullrush, Big Susan, Heartless, Lucy, Liza, Lousy Sall, and Shifty Jane (Porter 1969, 394).

THE FREE GARDENERS

Another example of an order with complex initiation rituals and symbolism is the Free Gardeners. This order was founded in Scotland in the seventeenth century. In 1873, John Hamilton, Master of the Glasgow Olive Lodge, defined its spiritual purpose: "Gardenery may be defined as the art of disposing the earth in such a manner as to produce whatever vegetables and fruits we desire, in large quantities and the greatest perfection of which their natures are capable. Free Gardenery is the applying of the cultivation of the ground and its productions as symbols expressive of the necessity of cultivating the mind in intelligence and virtue."

The oldest document of Free Gardenry, the minutes of the Haddington lodge of East Lothian, dated 1676, lists fifteen laws of the order, the "Interjunctions for ye Fraternity of Gardiners of East Lothian." This order was set up not by members of the laboring class, but by rich landowners who were interested in the design of formal gardens. It was thus a speculative order, like the Freemasons, who are speculative, rather than operative. At Dunfermline in 1716, another lodge was founded by the Marquess of Tweeddale and the Earl of Moray. It admitted speculative nongardeners from the beginning, being a charitable organization for the benefit of widows, orphans, and destitute members. Like those of the Orange Order, the lodges of Free Gardeners were sectarian, only Protestants being admitted as members. In 1796, three further aristocratic lodges were created: Arbroath, Bothwell, and Cumbnathan. Scotland at this time was still partly feudal, still based in part on the clan system, with serfdom common. Slavery was not abolished in the coal mines of Scotland until 1799. The slaves there were native Scots, not abducted Africans.

Independent of the aristocrats, but perhaps emulating their structures, working-class gardeners banded together as Free Gardeners to restrict their trade to men who had served apprenticeships, to promote their cause against their employers, and to support each other in time of need. As with earlier trade guilds and contemporary associations, the Free Gardeners developed their own rites and ceremonies, along with passwords and signs—"signs, secrets, and grips"—so that a brother could recognize a stranger as a member. As with all organizations, there were splits and schisms, and a number of different orders of Free Gardeners emerged. Eventually, many of them banded together under the aegis of a grand lodge, though some lodges refused to join and operated independently. Like some other trade-based friendly societies, the Free Gardeners often admitted nonpractitioners. And, as in Freemasonry, these speculative members diluted the original intention of the organization to maintain and promote the crafts of gardening.

In its heyday, the organization had more than fifty lodges in the Lothians, with a membership of around ten thousand. The organization declined in the twentieth century, affected by the two world wars and the economic depression that came between them. The original aristocratic lodges wound up after World War II, that at Haddington in 1953, and Dunfermline thirty years later. The charter of the grand lodge was taken to Cape Town, South Africa, in 1956, owing to the collapse of membership in Scotland and England.

The initiation rites of the Free Gardeners have features in common with many such associations. Here is one version of the apprentice's initiation. The candidate is divested of all means, minerals, and metals as well as parts of his clothing. His right breast is bared to show that he is not a woman, his left leg is bare, and he carries no metals nor money, so there are no weapons in the lodge. Blindfolded, he is led up to a door. He hears three knocks and is asked in whom does he put his trust. He is prompted to answer "God." Admitted, he is led around the lodge three times, two steps back, three forward "in order to show I would rather take three steps forward than two steps backward to the assistance of a brother in distress."

The candidate is then made to kneel, the explanation of which is "I was taught to kneel on my bare bended left knee, within three circles, on three squares of a gardener's apron: my left hand on the Holy Bible, Square, Compass, and Knife; my right hand extended toward heaven, holding the most useful, yet most dangerous implement of Gardenery, and my face due East. It was there I took that most solemn vow an obligation as an apprentice Free Gardener."

The vow makes reference to Adam being the "First Gardener." Adam was the first journeyman gardener, traveling the Earth in an attempt to restore horticulture to its pristine condition that it had once been in, in the Garden of Eden. The secret of gardenry was revealed only to Adam, not Eve, as in this questioning of the postulant:

"What did you come here upon?"
"My mother, Earth."
"What are you?"
"A man."
"How do you know yourself to be a man?"
"By having that revealed to me which was never
revealed to woman."

The candidate is then shown the emblems of Free Gardenry; the square, the compass, and the grafting knife, "the simplest tool of gardening," and the initiate is exhorted to "prune the vices and propagate the virtues by cuttings." He is then given the Gardener's Word. The Word of the first degree is *Dak,* probably meaning "delving and knowledge," and the password is *And:* "A meaning all things, for God made all things; *N,* nothing, for God made all things out of nothing; and *D* means dust, for "Dust thou art, and to dust thou shalt return" (a reference to Genesis 3:19). The third Word is Adam. There are signs associated with the second and third Words. The emblem of the apprentice is his apron.

The second degree of Free Gardenry is the journeyman, and the rites refer to Noah being the "Second Gardener." The initiation is a kind of pathworking, symbolically traveling to the Garden of Eden, finding the river that flows forth from there and divides into four rivers: Pison, Gihon, Hiddekel, and Euphrates—PGHE—from which derives the secret alphabet of the Free Gardeners. The next stage of the pathworking is to the Garden of Nuts, thence to Bethlehem, where the Star is seen. The working ends in the Garden of Gethsemane, the plant of renown, "Christ, our mediator and Elder Brother," Gethsemane being the garden planted by King David and King Solomon. The Word is Noah, who planted a vineyard and became drunk on the fruits, and the candidate is told to partake of drink but not in excess. The sign of the journeyman is having the heart plucked out.

The third degree makes reference to Solomon, the "Third Gardener," and to the symbol of the olive tree. The Word is Solomon and it has an associated grip. Solomon is called the "Third and Head Gardener," for he had knowledge of all the trees and shrubs and planted a garden in Balhama as well as tending Gethsemane. The Word is *olive*, and the associated sign symbolizes two olive leaves put together. The olive branch brought by the dove symbolized to Noah that God was reconciled with humans, the high priest of the Jews took an olive branch into the Holy of Holies in the Temple once a year, and Jesus went to the Mount of Olives to pray.

The Free Gardeners have their own regalia. Their aprons are of two types: long ones, reaching the ankle, embroidered with numerous emblems from the legends of the order, and short ones with a semicircular bib, resembling Scottish Masonic aprons. The apron of the president is embroidered with the letters *P, G, H, E,* the initials of the four rivers of the Garden of Eden, and *A, N, S,* the initials of Adam, Noah, and Solomon, to which is added the letter *O,* for "olive," and *TGGOTU,* the Great Gardener of the Universe.

There was some rivalry between members of rural fraternities. The song known as "The Painful Plough," or "The Ploughman's Song," talks of the rivalry between members of the Confraternity of the Plough and the Free Gardeners.

> *Come, all you jolly ploughmen, of courage stout and bold,*
> *That labours all the winter, in the stormy winds and cold;*
> *To clothe your fields with plenty, your farmyards to renew,*
> *To crown them with contentment behold the painful plough.*
>
> *Says the gardener to the ploughman, "Don't count your*
>   *trade with ours,*
> *Walk down in those fair gardens, and view those pretty*
>   *flowers;*
> *Also those curious borders, and pleasant walks to view,*
> *There's no such peace and pleasure performèd by the*
>   *plough."*

Says the ploughman to the gardener, "My calling don't
  despise,
Each man for his living upon his trade relies;
Were it not for the ploughman both rich and poor would
  rue,
For we are all dependent upon the painful plough.

For Adam in the garden was sent to keep it right,
The length of time he stayed there I believe it was one
  night;
Yet of his own labour, I call it not his due,
Soon he left his garden, and went to hold the plough.

For Adam was a ploughman when ploughing first begun,
The next that did succeed him was Cain, his eldest son;
Some of this generation the calling now pursue;
That bread may not be wanting, remains the painful
  plough.

Samson was the strongest man, and Solomon was wise,
Alexander, for to conquer was all his daily pride,
King David he was valiant and many thousands slew,
There's none of your brave heroes can live without the
  plough.

Behold the worthy merchant that sails on foreign seas,
That brings home gold and silver for those who live at ease;
With fine silks and spices, and fruits also, too,
They were all brought from the Indies by virtue of the
  plough.

Them that brings them over will find what I say is true,
You cannot sail the ocean without the painful plough,

For they must have bread, biscuits, pudding, flour and
  peas,
To feed the jolly sailors as they sails upon the seas.

I hope there's none offended with me for singing this,
For it was not intended for anything amiss;
If you consider rightly you'll own what I say is true,
There's no trade you can mention as can live without the
  plough.

The word *painful* would be rendered *painstaking* in modern English. There are a number of versions of this song. This one was taken down from the singing of Mr. Grantham, a carter from Holmwood, Surrey, and published in 1893 by Lucy E. Broadwood and J. A. Fuller Maitland (Broadwood and Maitland 1893, 126–27). Gertrude Jeckyll gives the final two lines of the last verse thus:

But if considered rightly, you will find what I say is true
That the wealth of the nation depends upon the plough."
(JEKYLL 1904, 191–92)

THE GENTLE CRAFT OF SHOEMAKING

Shoemakers were always regarded as being men with a philosophical character, becoming authors, songwriters, mayors, popes, and leaders in the vanguard of revolutionary social upheavals. Their patron saint is Saint Hugh, who, according to legend, was an ancient British nobleman, and hence the trade is considered noble and called the Gentle Craft. The other patron saints of shoemaking are Saint Crispin and Saint Crispianus, also noble Christian martyrs, whose day, October 25, is kept up by members of the Gentle Craft as the Shoemakers' Holiday. The sign of the Gentle Craft is Saint Hugh's Bones. A chapbook published in London in 1725, titled *The Delightful, Princely, and Entertaining*

History of the Gentle Craft, &c., printed for J. Rhodes, at the corner of
Bride Lane, in Fleet Street, tells us some of the shoemakers' Saint Hugh
legendarium. Hugh was the son of a pagan British king, Arviragus of
Powisland (Powys, Wales). But he fell in love and married a Christian
princess, Winifred of Flintshire, who converted him to Christianity.

Having given up his religion to become a Christian, Hugh was dis-
inherited. At once, he fell into poverty and was forced to learn a trade
to support himself, so he became a cordwainer (shoemaker). Then Hugh
preached by day and plied his craft by night. Both he and Winifred were
put to death during the persecution of Christians by the Roman emperor
Diocletian. Winifred was beheaded, and Hugh was forced to drink a cup
of her blood, mixed with cold poison, after which his body was hanged
on a gallows. However, he so loved his fellow shoemakers that, having
nothing else to give them, he bequeathed his bones to them. After his
skeleton had been "well picked by the birds," some shoemakers took his
bones down from the gallows and made them into tools. From then on,
shoemakers' tools were called Saint Hugh's Bones. They are listed in this
English shoemakers' guild rhyme, "The Shoemakers' Shibboleth."

> *My friends, I pray, you listen to me,*
> *And mark what Saint Hugh's Bones shall be:*
> *First a Drawer and a Dresser,*
> *Two Wedges, a more and a lesser.*
> *A pretty Block, Three Inches high,*
> *In fashion squared like a die;*
> *Which shall be called by proper name*
> *A Heelblock, ah! the very same;*
> *A Handleather and a Thumbleather likewise,*
> *To put on Shooe-thread we must devise;*
> *The Needle and the Thimble shall not be left alone,*
> *The Pinchers, the Pricking Awl, and Rubbing Stone;*
> *The Awl, Steel and Jacks, the Sowing Hairs beside,*
> *The Stirrop holding fast, while we sow the Cow hide;*

The Whet stone the Stopping Stick, and the Paring Knife,
All this does belong to a Journeyman's Life:
Our Apron is the shrine to wrap these Bones in,
Thus shroud we S. Hugh's Bones in a gentle lamb's skin.

Now you good Yeomen of the Gentle Craft, tell me how like you this?

As well (replied they) as Saint George does of his horse: for as long as we can see him fight the Dragon, we will never part with this poesie. And it shall be concluded, That what journeyman so ever he be hereafter that cannot handle his Sword and Buckler, his long Sword and Quarterstaff, sound the Trumpet, or play upon the Flute, or bear his part in a Three Man's song, and readily reckon up his Tools in Rhime, (except he have borne colors in the Field, being a Lieutenant, a Sergeant or Corporal,) shall forfeit and pay a Bottle of Wine, or be counted a Colt; to which they answered all viva, voce, Content, Content. And then, after many merry songs, they departed. And never after did they travel without these tools on their backs, which ever since have been called Saint Hugh's Bones. (Larwood and Hotten 1908, 283)

Fig. 6.2. The British shoemaker's emblem and motto.

Along with the shoemakers, the mythos of defleshed bones is significant among the toadmen and Bonesmen as well as being mentioned in the prospective doom of initiated Horsemen who break their solemn oath. "The Horseman's Creed" enunciates the punishment, "my body be quartered in four and swung in chains, and the wild birds of the air left to pick my bones, and these then taken down and buried in the sands of the sea, where the tide ebbs and flows twice every twenty four hours—to show I am a deceiver of the faith" (Neat 2002, 58).

A shoemaker being "counted a Colt" if he is unable to perform the tasks expected of him recalls young apprentices of the Confraternity of the Plough on Plough Monday in Cambridgeshire. First-timers, youngsters who had not been out before on Plough Monday, were called "colts." At Balsham, the whip men accompanying the plough were told, "Don't hesitate to touch up the colts when necessary" (Russell Wortley, interview with Bunny Brown, December 10, 1951). Also at Balsham, the colts had to pay for attending on Plough Monday, while the "old hands" did not. Before going out with the plough, the colts were first shod by having a nail driven into the sole of their boot. As the nail went in, to avoid injury, they were forced to call a halt to the nailing. Then the colt had to pay a forfeit of drinks all round. The connection of the colt's initiation with the boot is a link with the blacksmiths and shoemakers. At the Weyhill Fair in Wiltshire, there was an initiation rite called Horning the Colts, where a first-time attendee at the fair was sat in a chair in one of the village inns and forced to wear a cap fitted with a pair of horns. An initiation rite was chanted and then the initiate had to pay for drinks all round (Addison 1953, 150).

The Shoemakers' Holiday on the day of Saint Crispin and Saint Crispianus, who, like Hugh, were also noble Christian martyrs, on October 25, was kept up by members of the Gentle Craft. *The Shoemakers' Holiday, A Pleasant Comedie of the Gentle Craft* is also a seventeenth-century play written by Thomas Dekker. The text of the play begins with two "three-man's songs" (as mentioned in "The

Shoemakers' Shibboleth"), the second of which refers to Saint Hugh:
"The second three-man's song: This is to be sung at the latter end.

> *Cold's the wind, and wet's the raine,*
> *Saint Hugh be our good speede:*
> *Ill is the weather that bringeth no gaine*
> *Nor helpes good hearts in neede.*

> *Trowle the boll, the jolly Nut-browne boll,*
> *And here, kind mate, to thee:*
> *Let's sing a dirge for Saint Hughes soule.*
> *And downe it merrily.*

> *Downe a downe, hey downe a downe,*
> *I ley derie derie, down a down!*
> *Ho, well done; to me let come!*
> *Ring, compasse gentle joy.*

> *Trowle the boll, the jolly Nut-browne boll,*
> *And here, kind mate, to thee:*
> *Let's sing a dirge for Saint Hughes soule.*
> *And downe it merrily.*

> *Cold's the wind, and wet's the raine,*
> *Saint Hugh be our good speede:*
> *Ill is the weather that bringeth no gaine*
> *Nor helpes good hearts in neede.*

An old inn in London called the Crispin had the inn sign rhyme:

> *Here at the Crispin any man may for his money*
> *Immediately obtain shoes made out of animals' skins;*
> *But many a brute in this town wears a human skin,*

*Nay, wears his own brother's skin, and the brute looks
even well in it.*

(LARWOOD AND HOTTEN 1908, 282–83)

Until the late twentieth century, Northampton was the hub of shoe-making in England. The earliest record of shoemaking in the town is of Peter the Cordwainer, in 1202. June Swann, who was curator at the Northampton Museum, tells a story of having heard the legendary story of "sixty-four stitches to the inch" that was told about Northampton shoemaking craftsmanship. But during her time there, she had never actually seen an example of such refined workmanship until she received a shipment of nineteenth-century boots from the United States. In the United States after the American Civil War, many of the trades began to be industrialized. There was great resistance to factory work and wage slavery. Boot and shoemakers were among the most resistant, and their industry was, in fact, one of the last to be converted. During the late nineteenth century, prize work competitions were held to show that factory-made products could not compete with those made by hand by skilled shoemakers. Boots made in Philadelphia at such a competition were stitched with the legendary sixty-four stitches to the inch. The fin-est leather stitchwork that can be made with a modern sewing machine is thirty stitches to the inch. James Devlin says in his book *The Guide to the Trade* that this sixty-four stitchwork was done with an awl so fine that if a shoemaker accidentally pierced his hand, the wound neither hurt nor bled and that a needle only as thick as a human hair was used, giving rise to the saying that "a human hair was used for a needle."

BONES AND BONESMEN

In addition to the magic witch-bone procured by toadmen in going to the river and "The Shoemakers' Shibboleth," there are other local tra-ditions of bone magic in this region that may shed some light on the Ancient Order of Bonesmen. In 1851, the Northamptonshire folklorist Thomas Sternberg wrote, "Certain charms and amnulets were (and still are) resorted to in order to procure immunity from the arts of the witch. Among the most common of these was the 'lucky bone.' The *lucky-bone,* as its name indicates, is worn about the person to produce good-luck; and it is also reckoned an excellent protection against witch-craft. It is a bone taken from the head of a sheep, and its form, which is that of the T cross, may have, perhaps, originated the peculiar sanctity in which it is held" (Sternberg 1851, 150, 154). Sternberg also noted that in Northamptonshire, the patella (kneecap) of a sheep or lamb, worn as an amulet, is a remedy to ward off cramps. He mentions one instance he found of a human kneecap so used (Sternberg 1851, 24–25), which parallels the human knucklebones commonly believed to be carried by Bonesmen.

In 1911, the Peterborough folklorist Charles Dack wrote about a ritual performed in Huntingdon in which a skull was the main feature.

> Once a year, the Freemen of Huntingdon used to meet on the Market Hill; they then proceeded in procession, dragging a horse's skull with them and perambulated the bounds of the Freemen's lands. At certain points there are boundary holes dug, these holes they re-dig and hold a boy (one of the Freemen's sons) up by his

Fig. 6.3. Late eighteenth-century tombstone at St. Ives, Cambridgeshire, with a carving of Azrael, the Angel of Death, closing the lid of an urn containing a skull and bones. Possibly a Bonesman's grave.

heels with his head in the hole, and strike him (on the part prepared by nature for that purpose), with the spade. This is done at
each hole. A different boy was whipped at every hole so that several could remember where the holes were dug, especially the hole
at which each individual had suffered, and the memory of the hole
was impressed on mind and body, and the position of the boundary marks were thus registered. For many years the annual custom
has been discontinued, and takes place at irregular intervals. It has
only occurred once during this century. The men of Godmanchester
sometimes formed bands on the same day and when they met the
men of Huntingdon a free fight and struggle took place between
them to secure the horse's skull. (Dack 1911)

The Ancient Order of Bonesmen is the most secretive of all fraternities in this region. Members of the order have always been suspected
of practicing necromancy. Bonesmanry teaches that a certain residual
part of the spirit of the deceased person is present in any fragment of
his or her bone. So the ghosts of the dead can be summoned by playing
a tune on a whistle or flute made from human bone. The Bonesmen
warn that to burn human bones will cause bone-ache to the person
doing the burning. But, conversely, another tradition in East Anglia
tells how drinking ale containing the ashes of burnt human bones will
induce visions in the drinker. As operative practitioners, it is said that
Bonesmen were employed in laying skulls or bones in the foundations
and walls of buildings, having the proper knowledge of where best to
put them. Bonesmen laid floors of animal leg bones, embedded bones in
the chimney breast or the roof, and procured the bones needed, including horses' skulls. They seem also have been in the trade in bones for
grinding as fertilizer in bone mills such as that at Narborough on the
River Nar in Norfolk. Human as well as animal bones were brought to
be ground up at nineteenth-century bone mills in eastern England. The
mark of a Bonesman is one who carries a knucklebone of a sheep or
man as an amulet, ostensibly to prevent cramps. The sign of Bonesmen's

presence is three long bones laid side by side, one long, one medium, and one short, signifying the bone of a man, the bone of a woman, and the bone of a child.

As with other rural fraternities, the Bonesmen conduct fearsome initiations. The candidate is brought blindfolded at midnight on a Thursday to a graveyard. There, after he has been roughly handled and has sworn an oath, he is unhoodwinked and sees, by the light of burning brands, a pile of bones and a skull or perhaps an entire skeleton lying on a table tomb. On three sides of the tomb stand three officers of the order, the candidate making the fourth, and the skull and bones "the dead fifth." One of the officers, the senior warden, asks the neophyte to tell him whether the bones are the remains of a king, an earl, a freeman, or a beggar. The postulant cannot tell and eventually, after prompting, says so. To this, he receives the reply, "Whether he was a rich man or a poor man, they are the same now in death. So in life, the character of being human is the only one of any importance."

Fig. 6.4. Bone and lucky stone head, Hertfordshire.

He is then given certain teachings and the grip and password of Bonesmanry. It appears that many of these have never been revealed to noninitiates. New regalia must be made for each newly initiated Bonesman, and it must never be shown to anyone but a sworn Bonesman. When a Bonesman dies, he must be buried with his magic bones and all his regalia, never cremated. Among the few Bonesmen's secrets that have come out are some hand signals. For "no," the Bonesman puts the tip of his middle finger under his thumb, and flips it out. For "yes," the palm of the hand is turned outward, with its edge upward. For the sign that something is good, the Bonesman places a thumb on one cheek, his fingers on the other, and draws them down to his chin. The sign for something evil is made by spreading the fingers across the face, then dragging them off. By means of these and other hand signals, Bonesmen can communicate with one another without noninitiates knowing any communication is taking place (Pennick [1995] 2004, 64).

7

The Confraternity of
the Plough

*Witch-Men, n. Guisers who go about on Plough-Monday
with their faces darkened . . .*

Thomas Sternberg, *The Dialect and
Folk-Lore of Northamptonshire*

SPEED THE PLOUGH

Plough Monday is the first Monday after Epiphany. It is an ancient
custom observed mainly in the eastern half of England that still con-
tinues today. There are several theories about its origin, assuming it
has a single origin. One is that it was brought to England in the ninth
century by Danish settlers in continuation of the heathen tradition of
Midvintersblót, the day at the middle of the winter season. This might
have also commemorated the Danish celebration of victory over the
armies of Wessex in the year 878, which occurred "at midwinter after
Twelfth Night," which is Midvintersblót or Tiugunde Day, January 13,
twenty days after the Yule. The Danelaw, whose territory included this
region, was established in that year, and eastern England was under
Danish rule into the next century.

In 1851, Thomas Sternberg noted that in Northamptonshire the day was called "Witch-Monday" or "Plough-Witch-Monday" (Sternberg 1851, 123). In 1902, the Lincolnshire clergyman, folklorist and Viking enthusiast R. M. Heanley speculated:

> It is, I suppose, generally allowed that the Plough bullocks represent the Wild Huntsman and his rout. Be that as it may, at this season of the year great numbers of wild geese daily cross Marshland, flying inland at early dawn to feed, and returning at night. No one who has heard their weird cry in the dusk can feel surprised that the older labourers still speak with bated breath of the "Gabblerout" of the Wild Huntsman, and the wandering souls of children who have died without baptism whom he chases, and whom you may see for yourselves as "willy wisps" flitting across the low grounds most nights of the year. (Heanley 1902, 6, 7)

Another theory speculates that Plough Monday was established by the Archbishopric of York in the eleventh century. But it is clear that whatever other festivals have been attached to it, it is related to the return to work after the twelve days of Yule. In the early nineteenth century, it was generally accepted that Plough Monday was closely bound up with religious devotion. At the beginning of the nineteenth century, Francis Blomefield wrote, "Anciently, a light called the Plough-Light was maintained by old and young persons who were husbandmen, before images in some churches, and on Plough Monday they had a feast, and went out with a plough and dancers to get money to support the Plough-Light. The Reformation put out these lights, but the practice of going about with the plough, begging for money remains, and the 'money for light' increases the income of the village alehouse" (Blomefield 1805–1810, 9, 212).

In his *Norfolk Garland,* written in 1872, John Glyde Jr. tells of the medieval tradition of the confraternity of the plough.

Plough Monday was the name given to a rustic festival held on the Monday after the feast of the Epiphany, commonly called Twelfth Day, on which day, after the festivities of Christmas, it was in olden time customary to resume the labour of agriculture. There is in the tower of the church at Cawston a gallery called the Plough Rood, and on this the following lines are carved:

> *God spede the plow,*
> *And send us ale corn enow,*
> *Our purpose for to make*
> *At . . . of the plow lite of Lygate,*
> *Be merry and glad;*
> *What good ale this work mad.*
>
> (GLYDE 2008)

This is believed to refer to those celebrations of Plough Monday, which, prior to the Reformation, were not unusual in connection with guilds in agricultural districts. The members of the guild would go on Plough Monday to church, and kneeling before the Plough Rood would say: "God spede the plow, and send us ale corn enow our purpose for to make, that is, to carry on their labors on the land, and to spend a joyful day at the plow light of Lygate, and there to show their belief in the need of good ale to enable them to work, they say, 'Be merry and glad, 'twas good ale this work made.' After which they gaily dressed, passed in procession through the village dragging a plough that had been blessed and censed with incense by the priest, and gathered largess as they went along. It seems strange to us to pray for ale, but in those times ale was everywhere the common beverage of the country, and was thought as necessary for the support of life as bread, and therefore it was thought as natural to pray for ale corn to make ale with, as to pray for daily bread. Bread and ale gave them strength to plough the land" (Glyde 2008, 110). Its earliest historical record is in the sixteenth century.

PLOUGH MONDAY

Plough Monday was the traditional beginning of New Year's ploughing. It was marked by a procession of ploughboys and ploughmen around their local villages, dragging a plough. There are two related traditions, deriving respectively from regions where ploughing was done by oxen or by horses. In the northern and western parts of this region, Plough Monday is observed by bullockers, reflecting the use of oxen in former times. "Speed the Plough" is a traditional tune played by all musicians who participate in contemporary celebrations of Plough Monday and, since the 1970s, Plough Sunday, which sees the blessing of a symbolic plough by the clergy in church. From the eighteenth to the early twentieth century, Plough Monday was a boisterous time when boys and men in disguise walked their districts with a plough, dancing, singing, and demanding money, sometimes menacingly.

Fig. 7.1. Broom dancers, Mepal.

Early records of Plough Monday in this region are few. In 1684 in Huntingdonshire, two Fenstanton men, Thomas Martin and Emmanuel Offley, were arraigned for the manslaughter of John Banson of Little Shelford, who was riding across a shortcut across the Great Doles (certain kinds of fields in fenland) between Fenstanton and St. Ives when he was stopped for money, which he refused to pay. He was killed in the fight that ensued. The defendants claimed that it was customary on Plough Monday and Whitsuntide to take a penny from anyone who rode across the common land there (Tebbutt 1984, 55). Squire Payne paid money to the ploughmen on Plough Monday at Barnack in 1720 (Hart 1962, 67). At Fowlmere, William Cole was visited by the ploughboys on January 11, 1768, Plough Monday. "All the boys in the parish with Hurdy Gurdy's, black'd faces, Bells and Plows" (Frampton 1993, 6).

In the 1820s, the poet and musician John Clare wrote about the Plough Monday ceremonies at Helpston, north of Peterborough, where two separate groups went round—the plough bullocks, who took the plough round, and the plough witches, who "prided themselves in their disguise." The latter, who are the witch-men described by Sternberg, stuffed straw into their smocks to give the illusion of humped backs, and one of them, the she-witch, was dressed as a woman. The plough bullocks all blacked their faces while some plough witches did also. The She-Witch had his face "raddled." Both groups went round collecting money from the houses they visited. The common expression of "winding someone up" relates to the "wind up" of the Plough Bullocks, where the men used to attempt to trip one another up, tangled in the plough ropes.

Clearly, the Plough Bullocks wound up the authorities in many places. In 1821, the *Lincoln, Rutland and Stamford Mercury* reported, "Magistrates have determined to visit with exemplary severity the misconduct of persons who appear as morris dancers or Plough Bullocks or under any other name of similar character. The excesses of these persons have arrived at such a pitch that it would be impossible to bear them any longer, and it would be well if the country and the farmers in particular, would second the endeavours of the magistrates" (*Lincoln, Rutland*

and Stamford Mercury 1821). In January 1823, an irate correspondent in Basford wrote to the *Nottingham Review* to berate the bullockers.

It is a well-authenticated fact, that the Sabbath day and evening, previous to Plough Monday, are mostly spent in decking and besmearing the annual vagrants (for they certainly are no better,) called Plough Bullocks. The individuals, who thus disgrace themselves, generally sally forth, before daylight on the morning in question, amongst the peaceable inhabitants of the neighbourhood where they reside, and, in many instances, demand money with as little ceremony as the tax-gatherer. This year, there have been no less than five or six parties of these idle and disorderly persons in this village, who, not being satisfied with wasting Monday for such a bad purpose, have also included Tuesday; nor does the evil end here, for the money, which has been collected, is spent during the remaining part of the week in gluttony and drunkenness, and in nightly revelry and dancing. In fact, it is impossible to pass along the street when what is called the fool and witch are about, without being grossly insulted; and I have seen persons knocked down with a besom, besmeared with dirt, and even lamed by these impudent beggars . . . and I cannot but think, if our Magistrates have the power to stop this baneful custom, they would render an essential service to the community at large. (*Nottingham Review* 1823)

William Howitt, writing in Nottinghamshire in 1838, tells us:

Plough-Monday, here and there, in the thoroughly agricultural districts, sends out its motley team. This consists of the farm-servants and labourers. They are dressed in harlequin guise, with wooden swords, plenty of ribbons, faces daubed with white lead, red ochre, and lampblack. One is always dressed in woman's clothes and armed with a besom, a sort of burlesque mixture of Witch and Columbine. Another drives the team of men-horses with a long wand, at the end of which is tied a bladder instead of a lash; so that blows are given without pain, but plenty of noise. . . . They visited every house of any account, and solicited a contribution in not very humble terms. If refused, it was their practice to plough up the garden walk, or do some other mischief. One band ploughed up the palisades of a widow lady of our acquaintance, and having to appear before a magistrate for it, and to pay damages, never afterwards visited that neighbourhood. (Howitt 1838)

In Peterborough, gangs of ploughboys came into town on Plough Monday to call on the different tradesmen with whom their masters dealt, asking for presents. Charles Dack, writing in 1899, describes them:

These gangs of six or more were headed by a man. One boy was dressed as a woman, but all had their faces daubed with soot and red ochre, and dragged an old plough with a wooden share. In the country, if refused a present, the boys were yoked to the plough, and the path in front of the house ploughed up. In the town, the toe of the share was inserted under the scraper, and the plough-boys tugged, and away went the scraper. They were called Plough Witches and Mumpers. The leader used to repeat some doggerel, but I can only remember one verse, and unfortunately I have not been able to find anyone who can remember more. It was:

> *Look ye here and look ye there,*
> *And look ye over yander,*
> *And there you'll see the old grey goose*
> *A-smiling at the gander.*
>
> (DACK 1899, 4)

The ancient county town of Huntingdon faces its corresponding town, Godmanchester, across the Great Ouse River. Both Huntingdon and Godmanchester are on the Scottish drovers' easterly route, the Old North Road, and are linked by a medieval bridge. Huntingdon had its own tradition of dragging a horse skull around its boundaries, but it was in Godmanchester that the main observance of Plough Monday took place. In 1840, the *Cambridge Independent Press* reported a get-together at the Wheatsheaf in Godmanchester of six old men described as ploughboys, ranging in age from sixty-five to eighty-eight (*Cambridge Independent Press* 1840, 3). However, the custom was not restricted to old men, and this may have been a social gathering of superannuated ploughboys keeping up the day rather than an actual parade on the street.

But most Plough Monday observances were not carried out by frail old men. A comment in the *Lincoln, Rutland and Stamford Mercury* in January 1864 shows that Plough Monday celebrations were vigorously rambunctious.

> Ancient customs are all very well in their way, and so long as they are harmless in themselves and yet afford some little amusement and pleasure of association, let them survive; but some are indeed more honored in the breach than the observance. During the last few days a party of morris dancers or plough-jacks, or both combined, have made Barton their head-quarters, whence to radiate into neighboring villages, and a great "racket" they have made. In the evening the noise and uproar they made was a source of great annoyance, but they now appear to have brought the season to a close. (*Lincoln, Rutland and Stamford Mercury* 1864)

In Cambridgeshire, too, the press reports we have of nineteenth-century Plough Mondays are invariably disapproving. In 1855, the *Cambridge Chronicle* reported:

> The annual vagabondry of the plough witches took place on Monday, to the annoyance of a great number of the inhabitants. These witches principally represented themselves to be agricultural labourers from the neighboring villages, and disguised in women's clothes or with blackened faces, make pertinacious demands to all

they meet for money, entering your house with the greatest effrontery if they can do so unmolested. We really think that this custom would be more honoured in the breach than the observance; all responsible workmen now hold themselves aloof from the idle practice and it is confined chiefly to the lazy and the dissolute, against whom the police might swiftly put in force their authority for the quiet of the town. (*Cambridge Chronicle* 1855, 8)

In 1858, the *Cambridge Independent Press* reported:

Last Monday, some speculative labourers paid the inhabitants a visit in the character of a plough witch in order to get some little ready money for begging, but the plea did not act altogether in accordance with their wishes. They had not proceeded long before a police constable laid hold of one of them, who was dressed in a bonnet and petticoat and at the same time had a black face, enough to frighten some children, led him off in full trim to the police station. The effect was as magic as the water cure, for another fellow with a besom and a humped back of straw, made the best of his way to a place of safety. After some little time the man in custody was discharged, convinced that his profession would not take. (*Cambridge Independent Press* 1858, 7)

On January 2, 1865, George Davis, the chief constable, issued the following order to police superintendents in Cambridgeshire and Huntingdonshire: "Numerous complaints having been made as to the drunken disorderly, and in some cases, intimidating conduct of the mummers on the last year's Plough Monday, the attention of the respective Superintendents and Inspectors is directed to the suppression of the same on the coming occasion, and they will direct their several constables to caution the parties taking part in such proceedings that they are liable to be treated as vagrants, rogues and vagabonds, and in the event of disorder or importunity, will be proceeded against accordingly" (Frampton 1996, 9).

In the nineteenth century, at the beginning of each year, the local press stirred up a moral panic against Plough Monday. On Plough Monday in 1871, a thrown stone that broke a plate-glass window was blamed on the plough witches (*Cambridge Independent Press* 1871). The opinionated journalists of the Victorian press frequently called for the suppression of Plough Monday as a nuisance or worse. In 1873, the *Peterborough Advertiser* reported what the journalist perceived to be the dying observance of Plough Monday in Ramsey, which he called "this licensed system of begging and the attendant foolery of disguised villagers in the bloom of red-ochre, the sickly pallor of whiting, or the orthodox demoniacal tint of lamp-black" (*Peterborough Advertiser* 1873, 3). A record from Eye, to the east of Peterborough, in 1894, tells how then on Plough Monday "a large number of plough-boys attired in the most grotesque manner, having faces reddened with ochre or blackened with soot, waited on those known to be in the habit of remembering the poor old *ploughboy*" (*Peterborough and Huntingdonshire Standard* 1894, 8).

The press has not changed to this day, as the sensationalist tone of the mid-1800s can be recognized today in similar moral panics whipped up by journalists to boost their sales. In the twenty-first-century Cambridge press, one can read similar sentiments expressed by the police against the Strawberry Fair (*Cambridge News and Crier* 2010, 5).

Plough Monday traditions have clearly changed and developed over the years. Some customs have been dropped and others added. Tradition is a living thing. There are many elements in keeping up the day, not all of which may have existed at any one place. From Nottinghamshire, an 1886 report tells us, "Plough boys, plough bullocks or plough witches (for by all these names they are known), grotesquely dressed, blowing horns and drawing ploughs, perambulate on the first Monday in the new year (Plough Monday), and collect money for a feast. Mummers (now nearly extinct) perform a play in which is introduced the King of Egypt's daughter. Morrice dances are now almost a thing of the past" (J. B. 1886, 3). The Reverend R. M. Heanley noted in 1902 that at Wainfleet, Lincolnshire, "the

'Plough Bullocks' that are due on Plough Monday have ceased to carry with them the horse's skull" (Heanley 1902, 6).

In Hertfordshire, North Cambridgeshire, and Huntingdonshire, the participants in Plough Monday ceremonies are called plough witches (Jones-Baker 1977, 124; Tebbutt 1984, 52). Samuel Page Widnall, writing in 1875, described Plough Monday in Grantchester, near Cambridge: "Boys go round the village in a party of 30 or 40, and at each door shout in chorus 'Pray bestow a ha'penny on the poor plough boy—woa-ho-up,' repeated with a loud cracking of whips. Some of the young men go 'Ploughmondaying,' but they usually go into Cambridge for the day and make the round of the village in the evening. They deck themselves in ribbons and one of their number is dressed as a woman. A fiddler accompanies them and at intervals they stop in the street and dance, one or two going round to beg of passers-by. Only men and boys take part" (Widnall 1875; Porter 1969, 97). At Swaffham Prior, eight men making horse noises pulled the Plough Monday plough. At Whaddon, the six ploughboys serving as "horses" wore halters. A whip-man, who also held the collecting box, kept the horses in order, while the ploughman steered the plough behind.

In 1911, in his *Memorials of Godmanchester,* F. W. Bird wrote:

Sixty years ago, Plough Monday was a great institution in Godmanchester. Farming men, many of them dressed as women, and having their faces smeared, paraded the streets . . . they stuffed bundles of straw between their shoulders . . . they dragged a wooden plough behind them, and men, all more or less hideously attired, accompanied the procession with money boxes. They halted at each of the principal houses of the town, and asked for *toll,* pedestrians being solicited as they were encountered. If nothing was forthcoming from a call at a house, rumour said the plough witches made no more ado but forthwith ploughed up the front of the house and departed but no such damage was remembered in Godmanchester. (Bird 1911, 39)

Bird also noted that the plough witches at Godmanchester all carried besoms. The Plough Monday Horsemen and carters went round cracking whips at Bottisham.

As in Nottinghamshire in 1838, all over eastern England are records of what happened if a householder or farmer refused to give the customary "penny for the ploughboys." Either the front garden was ploughed up or the boot scraper by the door ripped out of the ground. At West Wratting, Billy Rash told Russell Wortley in 1960 that the ploughboys drew a furrow across the lawn of the big house in the village on one occasion when money was refused them. At Great Sampford around 1890 on Plough Monday, the Accordion Man was accompanied by the Pickaxe Man, who used his tool to dig up boot scrapers when requested, "Up with the scraper, Jack!" (Wortley 1972).

CUSTOMARY CHANTS ON PLOUGH MONDAY

Here are some customary chants:

General:

> God made bees,
> Bees make honey.
> Ploughman do the work,
> And the farmer takes the money.
> (JOHN THORNE, PERSONAL COMMUNICATION)

Pampisford:

> Up with your scrapers
> And down with your doors.
> If you don't give us money,
> We'll plough no more.
> (ORAL TRADITION)

Bottisham:

> I ninny nawney,
> Siftin' of chaff and a bottle of hay,

My poor nags go night and day.
Squeak boys, wag your tails,
A piece of puddin' and a piece of sow,
And if you don't give us something
We'll plough up your house.

The Shelfords:

Plough up your houses,
Plough down your doors,
Plough up the halfpenny,
For the little plough boys.

Harlton:

I'll plough up your hedges
And plough down your doors
If you don't give a halfpenny
To the Harlton ploughboys.

Foulmire (Fowlmere):

Plough Monday plough
Pudding in [the] sough
Plough up your scrapers
And down with your doors
Feel up the corner
You'll hear something jink
For we poor boys
Want something to drink.

Ickleton:

Plough Monday plough.
If you don't give us money,
We'll kick up a row.

Little Wilbraham:

Siftin' of chaff and a bottle of hay,

Make poor nag go merry away.
Sweep boys, wag your tail.

Great Wilbraham:

Ay ninny nawny.
Sifting of chaff and a bottle of hay.
Make your nag go night and day.
Squeak, boys, wag your tails.

(WORTLEY 1972)

TRADITIONAL CUSTOMS OF PLOUGH MONDAY

At Ramsey, where the Straw Bear presided over the festivities, it was the custom to settle personal scores on Plough Monday by playing practical jokes. This might involve ploughing up the garden or the front step, moving the water butt so it would flood the house when the front door was opened, or taking gates off their hinges and throwing them in the nearest dyke (Marshall 1967, 200–201). According to Bird, "severe encounters" between the Ramsey and Benwick plough witches "often took place."

The expression "the wooden spoon," a mocking award for a person who comes last in a contest, probably originates in a Cambridgeshire Plough Monday custom. Beginning in the 1820s and lasting until 1909, the custom was to present a wooden spoon to the Cambridge University student who scored the lowest marks in the examinations. This wooden spoon was a ceremonial object, painted with the coat of arms of the man's college. The custom arose at the time that degrees were conferred, January, the time when Plough Monday is celebrated. In some villages around Cambridge, the Fool, Molly, or Bessie collected money in a wooden ladle or spoon (Porter 1969, 100, 277). In a manuscript written in 1920 by F. L. Wales, she recorded that on Plough Monday at Little Shelford the last ploughman in the procession was the she-male guiser Bessie, who collected money in a wooden spoon (Wales 1920). So the wooden spoon was the symbol of coming last.

Fig. 7.2. Plough Monday molly dancing at the crossroads
in Comberton, Cambridge.

Disguise is a significant element of Plough Monday. The Cambridge
press of the 1850s has several references to the disguises of the plough
witches, who were "disguised in women's clothes or with blackened
faces" or "dressed in a bonnet and petticoat and hat and at the same
time had a black face." In 1888 at Elton, Northants, the day was kept
up by thirty men "dressed in fantastic costumes, some in women's
attire, others with large hats and streaming ribbons, and some with
darkened faces, paraded the streets" (*Peterborough Advertiser* 1888, 5).
Blackened faces are the common theme, being documented at St. Ives,
Eye, near Peterborough, Great Gidding, Kimbolton, Warboys, and
Yaxley between 1872 and 1940 (Frampton 1996, 17–18, 20–21). Plough
witches are recorded with blackened faces at Holywell around 1910, in
Easton up to 1939, and at Spaldwick in 1943. At Sawtry, faces were
blackened and coats worn inside out (Tebbutt 1984, 53).

Blacking-up is part of the Fenland molly dancing tradition in Cambridgeshire. In a typical account of Plough Monday from 1934, the *Ely Standard* noted, "Molly dancers attired in toppers, blackened faces and gaily-decorated uniforms paraded in many parts of the parish, singing and dancing over the broomstick" (Frampton 1994, 10). The landlady of the Anchor public house in Little Downham (1927–1940) blacked-up the molly dancers using candle-heated corks (Frampton 1994, 11). The Lady, a man in women's dress, had his face whited-up with flour (Reg Moore, quoted by Frampton 1994, 12). At Littleport in the early twentieth century, the Broom Man was called Humpty. He wore a tail made of braided straw hanging down his back (Porter 1969, 102). At Barnwell, a notoriously dangerous suburb of Cambridge on the Newmarket Road, where the Sturbridge Fair was held, it was said, "At night, too, a large number of these ugly ruffians black their faces and provided with large sticks, they beat at doors and calling themselves *Mumps* are clamorous for halfpennies" (*Cambridge Independent Press* 1851).

> *Mump, mump,*
> *If you don't give us a penny,*
> *We'll give you a good crump!"*

That was their chant. Mumping or lomping is associated more with Saint Thomas's Day, December 21, otherwise known as Dowlan Day. At Bottisham, lomping took place on Dowlan Day with the rhyme:

> *Lomp, lomp.*
> *If you don't give me something,*
> *I'll give you a good crump.*
> (WORTLEY 1972)

At Fulbourn, near Cambridge, in 1938 the molly dance accordion player Mr. Osborn told Russell Wortley that his father had told him about lomping, saying that in response to the chanted threat, people threw the lompers red-hot farthings that they had heated on a shovel in the fire.

At Haddenham in Cambridgeshire, the Plough Monday plough was bedecked with ribbons and greenery and was pulled by young men called "colts," who were driven by a man with a whip. First-timers, youngsters who had not been out before in the Plough Monday ceremonies in Cambridgeshire, were called colts as befitting the Horsemanry branch of Plough Monday. At Balsham, the whip men accompanying the plough were told, "Don't hesitate to touch up the colts when necessary" (Russell Wortley, interview with Bunny Brown, December 10, 1951). Also at Balsham, the colts had to pay for attending, while the old hands did not. In some places, the colts were first shod by having a nail driven into the sole of their boot. They were obliged to call a halt to the nailing to avoid injury, and the colt then had to pay a forfeit of drinks all round. Similarly, the spell against ague recorded from the Lincolnshire Fenland wise woman Mary Atkin involves nailing the sufferer's shoe. In the shoemakers' guild initiation, a shoemaker is "counted a colt" if he is unable to perform the tasks expected of him. Also, at the Weyhill Fair in Wiltshire, there was another initiation rite called Horning the Colts where a first-time attendee at the fair was sat in a chair in one of the village inns and forced to wear a cap fitted with a pair of horns (Addison 1953, 150).

In addition to taking round the plough, there is a particular form of dancing connected with Plough Monday—molly dancing. Villages around Cambridge—Comberton, Coton, Girton, Grantchester, Histon, and Madingley—had their own *sets,* that is, teams of dancers (Needham and Peck 1933, 2). The teams of dancers are usually referred to as molly sets or molly gangs. The sets left home early in the morning and danced at various locations, all ending up in Cambridge marketplace around midday, where they "danced against each other" (Needham and Peck 1933, 2–3). Each set had six dancers, one a she-male called the Molly or the Bessie, as well as a musician (in later years usually a fiddle or melodeon) and also the Umbrella Man. The umbrella is locally a sign of a cunning man associated with historical magicians of eastern England, including Cunning Murrell of Hadleigh and Old Winter of Ipswich. Accompanying the molly set in many places was a team of men dragging a wooden plough and men with whips that they cracked. In the evening, the sets returned to their home villages, where they drank and danced into the night. Women accompanied the men in these dances (Needham and Peck 1933, 3).

In 1911, Jonathan Clingo of Littleport (then aged eighty-five) recounted to the folk-song collector Cecil Sharp something of the former Plough Monday ceremonies, when the men then called morris dancers went round the villages nearby. One was dressed in woman's clothes, led by a man with a long feather in his cap and accompanied by a fiddler and a man with a broom. The dancers wore white shirts "with ribbons and scarves all over them and high box hats. . . . No bells, no sticks, no hand-kerchiefs" (Cecil Sharp's notebook in Clare College, Cambridge, cited by Needham and Peck 1933, 5). At Ely, the molly dancers wore ribbons on their sleeves and all down their trousers. Ely and Little Downham had a Tambourine Man who was also the Treasure Man (Bagman or Boxman) who collected the money. The Broom Man swept children off the dancing ground, and swept the snow if there was any. The men used to kiss Betty "and one thing and another" (Needham and Peck 1933, 5). In 1931, Frederick Shelton of the Little Downham set told Needham and Peck that it is "necessary to keep up the day." In 1932, the Little Downham set had six men, one of whom was the Betty and another who played a one-row melodeon. All had their faces blackened, and some wore goggles (Needham and Peck 1933, 6). In 1937, the *Ely Standard* reported that "Plough Monday was celebrated according to the old traditions. A party in fancy dress, armed with a broomstick and an accordion, paraded the village" (*Ely Standard* 1937, 13).

Sybil Marshall recalled in 1967 that at Ramsey the molly dancers of the early twentieth century put on the traditional disguise and used devil masks (Marshall 1967, 84), and in the Ely district, blackened faces and motorcycle goggles were worn in the early 1930s (Needham and Peck 1933, 6). In the late twentieth century, molly dancing split into two currents, with distinct forms of costume: the traditional, continuing the pattern described above, and a new form, with carnivalesque appearance. The traditionalists, with faces blacked-up, include the Old Hunts, Molly, the Old Glory Molly Gang, and the Good Easter Molly Gang, while the carnivalesque current is best characterized by the black-and-white Pig Dyke Molly and the multicolored Gogmagog Molly. In these latter sets, faces are painted in patterns or in multicolor.

8

Ritual Disguise and Resistance

WALTHAM, LITTLEPORT, CAPTAIN SWING, AND REBECCA

Blacking-up in the rural tradition has nothing to do with nineteenth-century minstrel shows, where white performers mimicked the imagined music and dance of slaves in the plantations of the United States. Blacking-up, covering the face with black material such as soot, lamp-black or burnt cork, is a ready form of disguise for light-skinned people. People engaged in clandestine or illicit activities in Britain have always resorted to camouflage. Poachers, walking by night, regularly blacked-up to minimize detection by the gamekeepers who were out to shoot them. In 1723, Parliament passed what is known as the Waltham Black Act, which sought to suppress unauthorized deer hunting in Windsor Forest and Waltham Close. The poachers blackened their faces to disguise themselves, and the act brought in the death sentence for those caught in such places armed and blacked-up (Schofield 2005, 13).

Of course, laws have never stopped the activities they seek to suppress, and despite the Waltham Black Act, poachers continued to use disguises, usually the havelock, a covering for the whole head and shoulders, with only two eye holes and a breathing-hole that was masked with muslin (Humphreys 1995, 167). Similarly, highwaymen frequently masked themselves. Contemporary gangsters, paramilitary operatives, and special forces soldiers wear the black balaclava. In their revolutionary attacks on machinery, tollgates, and oppressive farmers, the Luddites, Rebecca and Her Daughters, and followers of Captain Swing all blackened their faces, donned women's clothing, and used other disguises. The straw man was brought out for ran-tanning (for more on this, see chapter 13), the Straw Bear taunted the police, "Catch me if you can," and a man personating the devil oversaw rural initiations in barns at the dead of night.

The unwashed, blackened sweeps who paraded on May Day and the grimy miners and ironmen who danced what later became called the border morris were actually black-faced with industrial grime for most of their working lives. They did not need to black-up like the disguised poachers: this was their working condition. The plough witches blacked-up so that they would not be recognized by powerful people who could victimize them for their activities. The appalling conditions of the indigenous working class, both industrial and rural, in bygone days are today cleaned up by the heritage industry's reenactments that idealize life in the past. In earlier times, life was unimaginably hard by

Fig. 8.1. Masked highwaymen robbing travelers, eighteenth century.
The Library of the European Tradition.

the standards of Britain in the twenty-first century. Famines were frequent, the essentials of life were often difficult to obtain, and workers in fen and field often lived in grinding poverty at the edge of starvation. For example, in the first half of the nineteenth century, my ancestress, Elizabeth Hazelwood, living in Ely, Cambridgeshire, bore thirteen children. Nine of them died in infancy. Her experience was the norm rather than the exception in this region.

The starving farm laborers who took part in the Ely and Littleport riots of 1816 wore disguises. Militant workers in various parts of Britain have used the same forms of disguise during demonstrations and in their attempts to enforce solidarity during strikes. In the early nineteenth century in South Wales, strikers disguised themselves when they intimidated strikebreakers. The disguises they wore included blackened faces or masks, reversed jackets, cowhides, and women's clothing, items recognizable from the Plough Monday tradition. The Scotch Cattle traveled about as a "herd" of up to three hundred men, led by a "bull." Frequently, they were "flying pickets," men who came from a nearby town, so that the victims had less chance of identifying the members of the herd.

As they surrounded the cottage of a strikebreaker, in miner's strikes called a "blackleg," the members of the herd shouted, rattled chains, and blew cow horns. Usually, they then smashed windows and battered down the door, tore up sheets, curtains, and clothes, and smashed the furniture of the blackleg miner. If the butt of the attack resisted, he was given a heavy beating. In 1834, a miner's wife was murdered in an attack of the Scotch Cattle, leading to the execution of two of the perpetrators. Scotch Cattle also looted truck shops,* which claimed the monopoly of miners' supplies (Evans 1961, 48–51). The Scotch Cattle may have originated around 1808; by 1822, they came to the notice of those who wrote about such things, and the last recorded instance in the nineteenth century was in 1850. During the General Strike of 1926, some pickets in South Wales appeared as Scotch Cattle (Francis 1976, 232–60). The parallel with the

---

*A truck shop was a shop the miners had to use for their provisions, as they were paid in tokens that had to be redeemed at the truck shop, not in cash.

plough bullocks of Plough Monday in eastern England is striking.

In the winter of 1830 and 1831, farm laborers in southern England organized themselves into gangs to try to alleviate the harsh working conditions they were forced to endure. The rural followers of Captain Swing emulated the urban Luddites in destroying the machines that were taking away their work and rendering them destitute. Captain Swing's targets were the threshing machines. As well as campaigning for increased wages and better provisions for the poor, those under Captain Swing's banner sought justice from those who had oppressed them. They were known as "rural incendiarists" because their favored direct action was burning hayricks. Sometimes, though, they made direct attacks on the houses of the landowners and local landlords when they demanded food, drink, and money from their victims. Captain Swing, the generic insurrectionary name, like Jack Straw five hundred years before, sent letters threatening to burn down the barns and the "Blackguard Enemies of the People" within them. The movement was

Fig. 8.2. An 1830 cartoon of Captain Swing, legendary leader of the "rural incendiarists," disaffected farmworkers who attacked their masters' property. The Library of the European Tradition.

SWING!
taken from the Life.
Dedicated to Mess.rs Cobbett. Carlisle. &c C.º

suppressed with maximum force: six hundred were imprisoned, five hundred transported to Australia, and nineteen were executed.

The disguises adopted by the Scotch Cattle and Captain Swing and his followers were also used by Rebecca and Her Daughters in the uprising against road tolls in Wales in the counties of Pembroke, Carmarthen, Glamorgan, Cardigan, and Radnor, mainly in 1843. This took the pattern of a smaller attempt to destroy the toll system four years earlier. Times were hard for the ordinary people, and the exorbitant charges at the tollgates on the public roads were heavily resented. The rebels took as their motto a biblical text: "And they blessed Rebekah, and said unto her, Thou art our sister, be thou the mother of thousands of millions, and let thy seed possess the gate of those which hate them" (Genesis 24:60). Many of the rebels disguised themselves in women's clothing; some rode on horseback. Each group was led by a captain called Rebecca, his followers being known as "her daughters."

Rebecca and Her Daughters would arrive at night without warning, smash the gates with axes and hammers, and demolish the tollhouses after they had allowed the gatekeeper and his family to leave with their belongings (Molloy 1983). In June 1843, the insurgents entered Carmarthen in large numbers and attacked the workhouse to liberate the inmates, but were repulsed by a troop of cavalry that had been brought in from Cardiff. After this, the Rebeccaites became more violent. They expanded their attention to other grievances connected with the system of landholding and the administration of justice. Then "a state of terrorism quickly prevailed in the district." The government dispatched a large number of soldiers and a strong force of metropolitan police from London to South Wales, and the disorder was suppressed. In October 1843, a government commission was sent to Wales to inquire into the causes of the riots. Then Rebecca and Her Daughters were vindicated. The commission determined that their grievances were justified. Measures of relief were introduced immediately, and the tollgates in South Wales were abolished. The few Rebeccaites who were captured were only lightly punished. Their protest had achieved its objective.

An account from Scotland in 1877 showed blacking-up used in an act of resistance, which included an act of ill-wishing magic:

> Illicit distillation in the hills above Port Laire, near to Loch Torridon, has recently attracted the attention of the excisemen. After the officers had destroyed the apparatus they marched their prisoners to Inveralligan, where they were rescued by men and women with blackened faces. *The Scotsman* adds: "It is rumoured that a curious remnant of an old superstition is to be revived in connection with the seizure. A clay image of the preventive man is to be made, which, as the initiated well know, will cause him to waste away at the will of the artist. Donald may console himself with the reflection that he was experimented upon in the same way before, but to all appearance the 'corp criadha' had no effect." ("Superstition in the West Highlands" 1877, 163)

It is often said, without evidence, that blacking-up in British traditional performance originated in nineteenth-century minstrel shows, where white performers blacked themselves up to mimic African American performers. Because of this theory, blacking-up in traditional performance has become contentious in recent years, even involving police taking videos of morris dancers in the hope of prosecuting them (Schofield 2005, 12–14; Pennick 2005a, 30). This is in ignorance of

Fig. 8.3. A drawing of mummers in Oxfordshire, late nineteenth century, showing various disguises, including black face with glasses. The Library of the European Tradition.

records such as that from Fowlmere, Cambridgeshire, in 1768, which tell of "black'd faces, Bells and Plows" on Plough Monday (Frampton 1993, 6), and of the many other old accounts given here.

MINSTRELSY AND TRADITION

Minstrel show blacking-up began in Britain in 1836, when T. D. Rice, a white American, was a sensation at the Theatre Royal, Adelphi, in London for his rendition of a song-and-dance routine called "Jim Crow." Rice was blacked-up with burnt cork and wore a ragged costume mimicking the threadbare clothing of plantation slaves in the United States. Rice's performance began a craze for blacked-up performers to "jump Jim Crow" and sing what became known as plantation songs. Minstrel troupes from America soon followed Rice across the Atlantic to tour Britain. The banjo was thus introduced to Britain as a popular instrument. Today, a fretted version of the banjo is used mainly by folk musicians playing English, Scottish, and Irish music and in trad jazz bands. At that time, just before the Victorian era, audience tastes were having to change and get used to new types of entertainment because the more brutal entertainments such as cock fighting and bear baiting had been banned in the previous year. So there were openings for new genres of performance. Shortly after the minstrel craze took hold, ethnically black musicians became a feature of metropolitan Britain along with the blacked-up white minstrels.

Black military musicians have a history in the British Isles that goes back two hundred years before that. There is a tradition that the Scottish Life Guards had black trumpeters as early as the seventeenth century (*Notes & Queries* 1889, 448, 517). At the installation of the Knights Companion of the Order of the Bath in London in 1730, the fanfare was blown by twelve black trumpeters (*Notes & Queries* 1889, 237). From the early eighteenth century, slave bandsmen were recruited by the British Army from the plantations of the West Indies. These "sable musicians" were dressed not in standard uniforms, but in ornamental finery (Farmer 1950, 35). The old 29th Regiment of Foot had Afro-Caribbean drummers who were recruited in 1759, when the regiment was stationed in Kilkenny in Ireland. Slaves were brought to Ireland from Guadeloupe to play in the band. Colonel Enys records, "When I joined the regiment in 1775 there were three, if not more, of the original blacks in the corps, who were remarkable good drummers" (quoted in Edwards 1961, 20). Afro-Caribbean musicians played for that regiment for eighty-four years.

In 1783, the Duke of York brought black musicians to Britain from Germany, and in the 1820s, bandsmen were recruited directly from Africa, and African musicians became universal in the British Army, including the Household Cavalry and the Brigade of Foot Guards. But in 1844, Queen Victoria ordered that all of the black musicians should be thrown out of the army (Edwards 1961, 21). Unemployed and unemployable, many went on the streets as itinerant musicians, such

Fig. 8.4. The Ethiopian Serenaders, a troupe of black musicians in London in the mid-nineteenth century, formed after Queen Victoria expelled all black musicians from the British Army in 1844. Troupes of blacked-up white minstrels later used the same name. The Library of the European Tradition.

as the famous Ethiopian Serenaders, who worked fashionable streets in London. The influence of these black bandsmen remains today in the British Army; with great showmanship, the Afro-Caribbean and African drummers twirled their drumsticks dexterously. Called "the swinging of the sticks," this is still a feature of ceremonial military performance. The leopard skins worn ceremonially by Army drummers today are ascribed to the African drummers who served in the British Army in India in the 1840s (Edwards 1961, 20).

9

Witches, Wise Women, Quack Doctresses, and Cunning Men

CUNNING FOLK

At some point, the "Nameless Art" emerged as a way of talking about East Anglian magic. Cunning folk—witches, wise women, quack doctors and doctresses, cunning men, planet readers, charm sellers, horse doctors, Horsemen, toadmen, snakemen, initiated millers, alewives, wild herb men, and others of similar professions—always dealt with a nameless art that addressed various aspects of medicine, magic, and divination. There are multiple functions: to heal people and animals; to drive out evil spirits (exorcise) and lay ghosts; to communicate with spirits; to identify thieves and criminals; to find lost objects, animals, and people; to influence the weather; to interpret omens and tell fortunes; to enchant (exercise power over others); and to curse in various ways. The details of the rural magic practiced by these few recorded individuals remain largely unrecorded. There are a number of known oral transmissions of certain lore and techniques in East Anglia, but the overlap between what was transmitted in each case is not very large, and there is little to indicate a connected movement at any time. But,

121

as they say, "The function of the Nameless Art is to open up the way."

From all the accounts we have of cunning men and wise women, it appears that many of them used any and all techniques they could master. There is little to distinguish many from the conjurors, mountebanks, quacks, and flimflam men who traveled from fair to fair plying their trade; they used anything that would make them awesome in the eyes of those who had no idea about how it is done. These techniques were readily available to those who knew where to look. *The Art of Jugling or Legerdemain,* published in London in 1614, gave instructions valuable to any would-be cunning person.

> You must also have your words of art, certaine strange wordes, that it may not only breed the more admiration to the people, but lead away the eye from espying not of your conveyance, while you may induce the mind to conceive, and suppose that you deale with Spirits: and such kind of sentences, and odd speeches, are used in divers manners fitting and correspondent to the action and feat that you go about. As Hey Fortuna, Furia, numquam. Credo, passe passe, when come you, Sirrah? or this way hey lack, come aloft for thy maisters advantage, passe and be gone . . . Metmeltal, Saturnus, Jupiter, Mars, Sol, Venus, Mercury, Luna; or thus Drocti, Micocti, et Senarocti, Vein ba recti, Asmarocti, Ronnsee, Faronnsee, hey passe passe: many such observations to this art are necessary, without which all the rest are little to the purpose. (S. R. 1614, 10)

In his *Forty Years in a Moorland Parish,* the Reverend John Christopher Atkinson tells of a "wise man" known as Wrightson of Stokesley. Atkinson quotes "a Yorkshire Gentleman" who in 1819 gave a synopsis of the repertoire of this particular cunning man.

> Impostors who feed and live on the superstitions of the lower orders are still to be found in Yorkshire. These are called Wise Men, and are believed to possess the most extraordinary power in remedying

all diseases incidental to the brute creation, as well as the human race; to discover lost or stolen property, and to foretell future events. One of these wretches was a few years ago living at Stokesley in the North Riding of Yorkshire; his name was John Wrightson, and he called himself the seventh son of a seventh son, and professed ostensibly the calling of a cow-doctor . . . many came to ascertain the thief, when they had lost any property; others for him to cure themselves or their cattle of some indescribable complaint. Another class visited him to know their future fortunes; and some to get him to save them from being balloted into the militia, —all of which he professed himself able to accomplish. All the diseases which he was sought to remedy he invariably imputed to witchcraft, and although he gave drugs which have been known to do good, yet he always enjoined some incantation to be observed, without which he declared they could never be cured. (Brand 1827, 1905 quoted in Atkinson 1891, 111)

Those who have recently gained any powers often try to use them to influence and harm others. The powers of the cunning folk are ambiguous—as with all power exercised by humans—useful for life and healing, but also for illicit private gain and harm. The practitioner elicits both admiration and fear among those with whom he or she has business. Writing in 1825 about Messingham in Lincolnshire, John Mackinnon noted that

every misfortune and calamity that took place in the parish, such as ill-health, the death of friends, the loss of stock, and the failure of crops; yea to such a length did they carry their superstition, that even the inclemency of the seasons, were attributed to the influence of certain old women who were supposed to be in league, and had dealings with the Devil. These the common people thought had the power and too often the inclination to injure their property, and torment their persons. In early times it is much to be feared that many who were thought to possess the art of witchcraft, and lived in these retired villages, suffered greatly from the persecution of their ignorant neighbors. (Mackinnon 1881, cited in Gutch and Peacock 1908, 76–77)

As Catherine Parsons noted in 1952, "Witches liked to be credited with the power of evil so that the credulous would pay for protection and people's misfortunes would add to their reputation" (Parsons 1952, 45). However, perceptive commentators have always made a distinction between harmful witches and beneficial witches. In the second edition of his *A Glossary of Words Used in the Wapentakes of Manley and Corringham, Lincolnshire,* Edward Peacock gives the entry: "White Witch. A woman who uses her incantations only for good ends. A woman who, by magic, helps others who are suffering from malignant witchcraft. (Those who practice beneficial magic are, however, generally called wise-women, or wise-men)." (Peacock 1877).

THE CUNNING MEN

Cunning men who practiced during the nineteenth century are known from various parts of England. The typical repertoire of a cunning man is recorded well in the case of Elijah Dunn, "Dreamer Dunn," better known as the "Dudley Devil." He was a cunning man in the West Midlands who died in 1851. His first name may not have been Elijah, for "all prophets in the Black Country are 'Lijahs'" (Langley, n.d., 49). Dunn appears to have begun his career as a traveling fortune-teller, working from a booth at local wakes (fairs). There, he practiced under the name Seer Shaw and seemingly delivered his prophecies in rhyme. In 1817, an up-and-coming boxer, Tom Hickman, visited Seer Shaw and was told he would be very successful in the ring, but would be "crushed by coal." Hickman was a blacksmith and scoffed at the prophecy, as he had never entered a coal mine. In 1820, the now-rich Hickman, having made a fortune at prize fighting, was drunkenly driving his chaise and pair (a carriage with two horses) on the turnpike when he recklessly attempted to overtake a coal wagon. In the accident that followed, a wheel of the coal wagon fatally crushed the boxer's head. The fulfillment of Dunn's prophecy made him a local celebrity and brought plenty of clients.

Around 1850, another prize fighter, William Perry, "the Tipton Slasher," went to have his fortune told by Dunn (Langley, n.d., 50).

> *Slasher, you'll stop as you started.*
> *You'll get all you give'd in one go;*
> *You and your pub will be parted,*
> *Tom Little will make it come true.*
> [rewritten in standardized English—NP]
> (LANGLEY, N.D., 55)

The prophecy is said to have foreseen Perry's brutal defeat in 1857, six years after Dunn's death, at the hands of Tom Sayers, who, though of small stature, was a formidable boxer who left Perry brain damaged and unable to fight again. Dunn appears to have prophesied more generally as well as telling fortunes for individual clients. In the 1840s, Tom Langley tells us, a schoolmaster asked Dunn to prophesy what life would be like in two hundred years' time.

> *So quickly will they travel*
> *That there'll be no 'ere or there.*
> *They'll pass by the moon in a bullet*
> *And live on cold cloud and hot air.*
> (LANGLEY, N.D., 62)

In addition to telling fortunes and prophesying the future, the Dudley Devil was a typical cunning man who made a living prescribing "charm cures" for ailments such as toothache and gout, and also practiced thief-finding divination. The remedies had a Christian religious basis, such as the charm against toothache, which recalls Saint Peter being cured by Jesus: "Peter sat at the gate of Jerusalem, Jesus passed by and Jesus said . . . 'What ails thee, Peter?' Peter said unto Jesus . . . 'My teeth ache and are sore. I am unable to stand or to walk!' Jesus said . . . 'Arise and walk, Peter, in the name of the Father, Son and Holy Ghost. He that puts faith in these words I now spake, his teeth shall never ache" (Anonymous 1977, 39). Dunn sold this charm, which had to be put in a small leather pouch and worn close to the sufferer's body. The charm only worked as long as the sufferer had strong faith.

Many traditional magical charms have the names of Christian divinity in them as words of power. The spells probably came from a particular magic book, several of which were circulating at that time. For example, the *Romanus-Büchlein,* which circulated in eighteenth-century Germany, was taken to the United States and ended up translated and published in the mid-nineteenth century as *The Long-Hidden Friend,* and it contains medical remedies that are mainly spells (Brown, Hohman, and Hohman 1904, 89–152). Langley tells that in the 1840s, his great-grandmother went to Elijah Dunn to find out a thief who was taking money from the drawer (the forerunner of the till) at the Borer's Arms pub that she and her husband ran. She was told to look long at the liquor bottles on the top shelf and allow no one to touch them until she went to bed. The next morning, she looked behind them, and there was the money.

Despite his epithet "Devil," Dunn was buried in the Netherton churchyard, and for many years his grave was kept clean, though he had no known relatives (Langley, n.d., 62). He was buried in consecrated ground despite the local rumor that he had a contract with "the Black'un." Another famous cunning man was Hodges of Sedgeley, close to Dudley: "When I lived at Kidderminster, one of my neighbours affirmed that, having his yarn stolen, he went to Hodges (ten miles off) and he told him that at such an hour he should have it brought back home again and put in at the window. So it was, as I remember the story, Hodges showed him the face of the thief in a glass. Yet—I do not think that Hodges made any known contract with the Devil, but thought it an effect of art" (Richard Baxter, quoted in Anonymous 1977, 39).

According to Atkinson, who devotes several pages to him in his memoirs, the wise man Wrightson of Stokeley, despite being condemned as a charlatan by some,

> possessed, in common with many others then and since, wide and deep acquaintance with herbs and simples, and he used his knowledge with skill and judgment. No doubt also he knew the properties and uses of what we more usually speak of as "drugs," and employed them accordingly. No doubt either that he possessed the power of influencing men's minds and imaginations, and knew it right well, and used it of set purpose and intention; and heightened it, moreover, by the mystic means he had at his command, and knew how to render serviceable on occasion and with sufficient impressiveness. But grant these particulars frankly, it must yet be admitted that he had much and effectual machinery available, other than what is implied when we style a man a "rank impostor." (Atkinson 1891, 113)

The powers employed by cunning men were real, even if they were not always what they appeared to be. The power of compulsion is attested to in some accounts of cunning men. Master Fidkin at Arley, Herefordshire, put people under a spell that made them wander the village all night (Palmer 1992, 154). Old Winter of Ipswich caught a man stealing wood from a woodpile and compelled him to carry the load on his back, walking in circles until he collapsed. Another man, caught stealing cabbages from Winter's garden, was compelled to sit in the cabbage patch all night, immobile. Many similar stories are told of the nineteenth-century Herefordshire cunning man Jenkins, known to have the ability to find lost property and to identify thieves (Leather 1912, 57–59). As Atkinson notes, "The most lucrative part of the Wise Man's 'practice' seems to have been connected with the recovery of stolen or otherwise lost goods" (Atkinson 1891, 120).

In the 1840s, a man known as the Wizard of Lincoln was employed to find thieves.

A robbery having been committed at a farm, and no clue being found, though several persons were suspected, the farmer's wife persuaded her husband to send for the wizard of Lincoln, named Wosdel, who came with his familiar spirit in the form of a blackbird, and soon found out who had committed the robbery, and how it was done; but in doing so the fluttering about in the crewyard, under Wosdel's direction, so terrified the cattle that a labourer had the greatest difficulty in keeping them out of the barn where he was threshing. Then the wizard asked the farmer and his wife whether he should make the two thieves come into the room at once or show them on the wall, and on their saying he might do which he pleased, a labourer hurried into the room to ask what he was to do, though he had been told his work just before. When he was gone, Wosdel said, "That is one of them, and that" (pointing to the figure of one of their farm lads, which appeared on the wall) "is the other." Soon after, the man and lad were arrested, and the man turning king's evidence, and the money being found concealed at the lad's home, he was convicted and transported. (Gutch and Peacock 1908, 84)

A magician of repute named George Pickingill died at Canewdon in 1909. According to the writer Lugh, who claimed to be a hereditary witch, indeed a "witch-master," Pickingill, from Hockley in Essex, founded nine covens of witches in East Anglia and southern England (Lugh 1982, 3; Gwyn 1999, 19). Pickingill had a reputation for menacing people with threats of magic for financial gain. He is alleged to have influenced the prominent twentieth-century magician Aleister Crowley (Lugh 1982, 5–6), but his influence on contemporary Wicca is disputed. If Pickingill did set up autonomous covens outside his own village, it may have marked the beginning of speculative witchcraft, which, later in the century, under the influence of the writings of Margaret Murray, transmuted into a religion.

James Murrell of Hadleigh in Essex, who was born in 1812 and died in 1860, was a shoemaker by trade. But he was known widely as Cunning

Murrell because he was a cunning man. Murrell traveled only by night, and his accoutrements included a basket of herbs gathered in the light of the moon and a "brolly," a gingham umbrella (Howe 1956, 140). The umbrella is a "badge of recognition" of cunning men, carried at all times furled, whatever the weather. The "Brolly Man" appears nowadays with some molly dance gangs. After Murrell's death, letters were found written to him by people from as far away as Suffolk and London, asking him for advice (Howe 1956, 139). Murrell's specialty was to treat sick animals with herbal remedies, to recover stolen horses or cattle, and to perform countermagic against those whom his clients believed had bewitched them, for he claimed to be "the Devil's master" (Howe 1956, 138). To do this, he used an iron bottle that he filled with parings of horses' hoofs, pins, and chemicals. It was then welded shut by a blacksmith and put on a fire until it exploded, thereby eliminating the ill-doer (Howe 1956, 139). This technique was published by Joseph Glanvil in 1689 in his *Sadducismus Triumphatus*.

Writing in 1877, Edward Peacock noted that in Lincolnshire:

> It is still a common belief that, if you are bewitched, and you get some human hair, urine, and pins, and put them into a bottle and bury them under the eaves of your house, the witch will cease to have power over you. If an animal has been killed by witchcraft you must take out its heart and stick it full of pins, and either bury the heart in a box or earthen pot under the eaves of the house, or boil it in a pot over the fire; the witch will then have no further power. At a place on the west side of Hardwick hill, on Scotton common, I have been informed there was, sixty years ago [i.e. about 1817], "a great heap" of pins and old-fashioned tobacco-pipe heads; they were believed to have been put there for magical purposes. (Peacock 1877, 193)

One of the reasons people went to cunning men and wise women was to find lost objects, and well into the nineteenth century, techniques of divination were also used to find corpses of people drowned in rivers. Magical techniques were used, often given a rational explanation that nevertheless does not explain the result. "About the year 1827 a boy named Dean was drowned whilst bathing in the Thames, as it flows by the playing fields of Eton College" a correspondent to *Notes & Queries* noted in 1886. "The body was dived for, but could not be found. Mr. Evans, the well-known drawing-master, arrived on the spot, and having ascertained whereabouts the boy disappeared, he threw a cricket-bat on the place, which floated with the stream until it stopped in an eddy, where it began to turn round. The eddy was caused by a hole in the bed of the river, and, lying at the bottom of the hole, the body was found" (*Notes & Queries* 95, January 1886). In the *Stamford Mercury,* December 18, 1885, is a report of an inquest into Harry Baker, age twenty-three, who fell into the river on November 27 of that year. His mother prepared "a loaf charged with quicksilver (said to be scraped from an old looking-glass)." She threw the loaf into the river, and it came to a standstill at a certain place where the body was found. Corpse finding by floating objects behaving in an unusual way is quite similar to the means of selecting the witch-bone in the toadmen's toad-bone ritual.

WITCHCRAFT AND FOLK MAGIC

By the eighteenth century, courts were becoming less likely to sentence people for being witches; the last execution for witchcraft at Northampton was in July 1712. In the year 1734, capital punishment for witchcraft was abolished in England, though witchcraft continued to be legally a felony. Most of our records of traditional country witches come from the time after this. Strange tales attach themselves to noteworthy places. A common story is that in particular villages "the office of witch" is a permanent one and must be handed on to a successor. In Cambridgeshire, it is told that at Horseheath and Bartlow witchcraft is hereditary (Porter 1969, 161), where the power is passed from father to son or mother to daughter (Howe 1952, 23). In Essex, the village of Canewdon is often called "the village of witches," where there are said to be always living six (or nine) witches (Howe 1952, 23). Henry Laver, writing in 1889 of Essex fifty years earlier, remembers Mother Cowling, "an old harmless woman at Canewdon who was credited with the possession of fearful powers" and was blamed for others' ills (Laver 1889, 29). Some women handled this reputation by denying everything, while others profited from people's fears, using them as a source of income.

Writing about Lincolnshire in 1898, J. J. Hissey recalled a meeting with

> a clergyman I met on the journey and who confided in me said, "To get on in Lincolnshire, before all things it is necessary to believe in game, and not to trouble too much about the Catholic faith." He further assured me as a positive fact that both devil-worship and a belief in witchcraft existed in the county. He said, "I could tell you many strange things of my rural experiences," and he did how the devil is supposed to haunt the churchyards in the shape of a toad, and how witchcraft is practised, etc. "You may well look astonished," he exclaimed, "at what I tell you, but these things are so; they have come under my notice, and I speak advisedly from personal knowledge." (Hissey 1898, 223)

Until 1953, when it was destroyed in the disastrous East Coast floods, Duval's House, or Devil's House Farm on Wallasea Island near Canewdon was the reputed former dwelling of a certain Mrs. Smith, otherwise known as Old Mother Redcap. James Wentworth-Day records an account by Alfred Herbert Martin, a farm laborer who worked on the island for more than forty years. He claimed to have seen Mrs. Smith crossing the water to the island on a hurdle as if it were a boat. As she peeled potatoes, Martin claimed, Old Mother Redcap chanted "Holly, holly, brolly brolly, Redcap! Bonny, bonny" (Wentworth-Day 1973, 39).

We are fortunate that on February 1, 1915, a local woman, Catherine Parsons, read a paper before the Cambridge Antiquarian Society detailing current witchcraft in and around the Cambridgeshire village of

Horseheath. In 1952, she detailed further material in a manuscript that has never been published (Parsons 1915; 1952). "In Horseheath witchcraft is by no means a lost art," she said. "One is told that the chief difference between a witch and an ordinary woman is, that if the latter wishes her neighbor misfortune, her wish has no effect, but the same wish in the mind of a witch has effect, because the witch is believed to be in league with the devil, she having made a contract to sell her soul to him in return for the power to do evil."

A woman known as Daddy Witch is recorded by Parsons (Parsons 1915; 1952). Living in Horseheath, Daddy Witch "gained much of her knowledge from a book called *The Devil's Plantation*" (Parsons 1915, 39). This book is unknown, and has not turned up yet, despite years of searching. Its name refers to the eerie uncultivated "no-man's land" at the corners of fields. When she died, as an outsider she was buried in the middle of the road, not the churchyard. Another witch at Horseheath, supposed to have died in 1926, was known by the generic witch-name Old Mother Redcap. The name Red Cap appears among the Horseheath Imps, supposed to be kept in a box in the village (see chapter 10, page 138) (Parsons 1915, 34).

The Mother Redcap is an old inn name that occurs in various places. Larwood and Hotten, in their monumental study, *The History of Signboards from the Earliest Times to the Present Day,* tell of this name in London in "Upper Holloway, in the High Street, Camden Town, in Blackburn, Lancashire, in Edmund's Lowland, Lincolnshire, &c. . . . Who the original Mother Redcap was, is believed to be unknown, but not unlikely it is an impersonification of Skelton's famous 'Ellinor Rumming,' the alewife" At Holloway, the Mother Redcap once had the following verses on its signboard:

> *Old Mother Redcap, according to her tale,*
> *Lived twenty and a hundred years*
> *By drinking this good ale;*
> *It was her meat, it was her drink,*
> *And medicine besides,*

And if she still had drank this ale,
She never would have died."

(LARWOOD AND HOTTEN 1908, 96)

For an alewife with a knowledge of brewing and a mistress of the brewer's Word, the name Mother Redcap may have been a title. Until the professionalization of medicine, handywomen served as midwives and dealt with the dying, sometimes performing mercy killings. There were also women who practiced medicine, though it was only legal for men who had attended Oxford or Cambridge Universities to do so. In 1818 William Johnstone White drew the picture reproduced here of the "Quack Doctress," Ann Manning, being consulted by the market woman, Elizabeth Ayton, who died shortly afterward. White made this engraving to demonstrate the need for dispensaries to be set up in towns so that the poor would not be forced to use English traditional medicine. Women such as Ann Manning were common in rural districts in the nineteenth century. In 1851, Thomas Sternberg wrote, "There are few villages in Northamptonshire, the Southern district especially, which are not able to boast a professor of the healing art, in the person of an old woman, who pretends the power of curing diseases by charming" (Sternberg 1851, 153).

Fig. 9.1. Quack doctress Ann Manning with a client, market trader Elizabeth Ayton. William Johnstone White etching, 1818.

10

Handywomen, Witches, and Witchcraft

HANDYWOMEN AND EUTHANASIA

The precise boundary between witches and handywomen was always uncertain. In 1512, a law had been imposed making midwifery illegal without a license from the local bishop's court, and in 1518, the College of Physicians had attempted to monopolize midwifery. Until the early twentieth century, however, a handywoman, often called the nurse, was the village midwife who prescribed various remedies for illnesses and disorders and assisted in childbirth. Handywomen also assisted the death of those who were considered without hope of recovery. Handywomen were abortionists as well as midwives. They prescribed various abortifacient herbs to terminate unwanted pregnancies. Rue tea was a favorite. Toads, associated in the popular mind with witchcraft and toadmanry, were used by Fenland handywomen in an attempt to cure breast cancer. The handywoman would catch a toad and rub it until it swelled up and exuded venom from the warts on its skin. Then it would be rubbed on the tumor until no more venom was produced. The tumor was then covered with a plaster of houseleek (Porter 1969, 75). Another attempted cure of cancer was to rub the patient's face with a dead woman's hand (*Peterborough Standard* 1899).

In the days before police forces and forensic science, mercy killing was an option for those who were beyond hope of recovery and suffering intolerable pain. Usually, there was nothing suspicious in the death of someone who was already dying, and the chance of a mercy killer getting punished was minimal. People bitten by mad dogs, doomed to die in agony of rabies, were suffocated by having a pillow held over the face. There is an account of a trial of those who did this in the *Dublin Chronicle* for October 28, 1798, but euthanasia in this way was by no means restricted to Ireland. In the Cambridgeshire Fens, euthanasia was carried out by handywomen until early in the twentieth century. Of course, because it was carried out in secret, there are few accounts of the procedure, for the punishment for performing euthanasia was hanging.

In 1958, Enid Porter published details of what was called "snatching the pillow," which was the name for euthanasia conducted in the Fens. It was done at Littleport near Ely until 1902. In 1910, W. H. Barrett was told the technique by a woman, once a village nurse and midwife, who had performed mercy killings. The handywoman would be summoned to the house of a person who was to be killed. She carried a special pillow through the village, and people kept indoors and drew their curtains while she walked. At Littleport, the pillow was handed down to each successive handywoman. It was covered in black lace and said to have been made by a nun at Ely.

When the handywoman arrived at the house, she was given a glass of gin. Then she crushed two opium pills to powder and mixed them with gin and administered the mixture to the patient. According to Barrett, the patient was then propped up on the pillow, and the pillow was pulled away, causing death. But as earlier accounts tell of suffocation, it is more likely that the patient was suffocated. Only the handywoman was in the room with the patient, so nobody else saw what she did. In Littleport, the last handywoman to snatch the pillow was Mrs. Feltwell. When she died in 1902, her son burned the pillow and the practice was not handed on to Feltwell's successor (Porter 1958, 119).

As with snatching the pillow, there are relatively few accounts of what wise women or witches actually did. One detailed account, from the northern part of the Fens, in Lincolnshire, shows the similarity of the wise women's craft to that of the cunning men.

> It [the following charm] was communicated to me by that "wise woman" Mary Atkin. . . . In the autumn of 1858 or 1859, I forget which, the ague was particularly prevalent in the Marshes and my mother's stock of quinine a thing really wise Marshfolk were never without in those days was heavily drawn upon by the cottagers. But on taking a second bottle to Mary's grandson the old dame scornfully refused it, saying she "knawed on a soight better cure then yon mucky bitter stuff" [standard English: knew of a much better cure than that mucky bitter stuff]. And with that she took me into his room and to the foot of the old four-poster on which he lay. There, in the centre of the footboard, were nailed three horseshoes, points upwards, with a hammer fixed cross-wise upon them. "Thear lad," she said, "when the Old 'Un comes to shaake 'im yon ull fix 'im as fast as t' chu'ch steeaple, he weant nivver pars yon." And when I showed signs of incredulity she added, "Nay, but it's a chawm. Oi teks the mell 'i my left hand, and Oi taps they shoes an' Oi says,

> > *Feyther, Son and Holy Ghoast,*
> > *Naale the divil to this poast.*
> > *Throice I smoites with Holy Crok,*
> > *With this mell Oi throice dew knock,*
> > *One for God*
> > *An' one for Wod,*
> > *An' one for Lok."*

Mary Atkin took a hammer in her left hand and tapped the shoes' nails, saying the charm. There has been much speculation about "one for Wod" and "one for Lok," Wod being interpreted as Woden and the other Loki, though "one for luck," although perhaps a relic of not forgetting to invoke Loki, also just means to ensure luck in the action. This spell is to bind "the Old 'Un" who is deemed responsible for giving the ague sufferer the shakes (Gutch and Peacock 1908, 125).

At Longstanton in Cambridgeshire, toward the end of the nineteenth century, the local woman reputed to be a witch was Bet Cross. She played tricks on people, including stopping horses that were going past her garden, the classic technique of the horse whisperer. After she died, someone recalled seeing her flying on a *hardle* (hurdle), recalling the story of the Essex Old Mother Redcap and the witch from Withersfield (Parsons 1915, 39). The person who told the tale, in this case literally a friend-of-a-friend story, claimed that Cross had warned him, "You can tell on it when you think on it." This gave rise to a Longstanton adage, "You can tell on it when you think on it, and you know when that'll be" (M. G. C. H. 1936, 507; Porter 1969, 172). Such events are remembered when the person dies, for they should never be told while the person lives.

In 1915, the Horseheath Imps were still in the keeping of a woman

Fig. 10.1. Mummified toads from Cambridgeshire and Suffolk.

from Castle Camps. "Their present owner," wrote Catherine Parsons, "received them from her sister D. We are told that when this poor creature was dying, no one could stay in the room with her on account of the sulphur, which came from her nose and mouth." Such is the imagination of Castle Camps folk. But it was said that D. would never have died had it not been for the woman who was nursing her, whom D. had cautioned not to open a certain hutch in her room, or she would die, but the old nurse turned a deaf ear to the caution, being overcome by curiosity to examine a certain red underskirt kept in the hutch, in which the imps had been wrapped. It is said that our imps were brought to Horseheath in a box, on which the owner sat during the journey. Although the box was securely corded, no one was allowed to touch it, not even in assisting to lift the box in or out of the cart, for imps are curious creatures, and no cords or even iron bars can keep them in bounds unless they are solely under the control of their owner.

Parsons recounted the names of the Horseheath Imps:

> five in number . . . Bonnie, Blue Cap, Red Cap, Jupiter, and Venus. As to their appearance opinions differ, but they are generally said to be something like white mice. Mrs. B. has described one sitting on top of a salt box in old Mrs. C.'s chimney corner, as being something like a mouse, with very large eyes, which kept getting large, then small. . . . It was believed that this particular imp had been sent down the chimney to see what was going on in the cottage, in order to report any item of interest to the witch, for it is useless trying to conceal anything from a witch. What one does not choose to tell, can always be discovered by the parish witch or wizard with the aid of an imp. (Parsons 1915, 33–34)

At Willingham, on the edge of the Fens, Jabez Few, who died in the late 1920s, used his white rats to terrify gullible villagers who called them his imps, playing tricks like Bet Cross of nearby Longstanton (Porter 1969, 175–76).

The details of the rural magic practiced by these few recorded individuals are largely unrecorded. There are a number of known oral transmissions in East Anglia, but the overlap between what was transmitted in each case is not very large, and there is little to indicate a connected movement at any time. Those accounts of witches that contain any personal details show that most women reputed to be witches lived on the margins of society and were among the most impoverished in their respective villages. A description of the Burwell witch Old Judy in 1888 tells that she lived in the most northerly of the squatters' cottages, which were "half a dozen primitive one-storied hovels built of wattle-and-daub with clunch chimneys thatched with sedge and litter" (Porter 1969, 161). In Horseheath, Daddy Witch was "half-clothed in rags" and "lived in a hut by the sheep-pond at Garret's Close" (Parsons 1915, 39).

ANIMAL STOPPING

The most impressive of powers exercised by Horsemen, toadmen, and witches was the stopping of animals. There are many stories of this power being exercised and of the astonishment or exasperation of those who could not make their horses move again. Around 1830 at Wisbech was "an old witch who could stop horses on the road and not let them go on until she liked" (Bales 1939, 69). A story from Upwood in Huntingdonshire, related in 1927, tells how a farmworker was bringing home a load of wheat when his wagon stopped unexpectedly at a certain place and the horses refused to move. An old woman came out of the cottage nearby, picked up a straw that was lying in the road, and then the horses proceeded without difficulty (Tebbutt 1984, 84–85). The straw in the path—the brandon—is an ancient symbol of a closed passage, and here it was more than symbolic. It is clear that the straw was doused in an active substance, perhaps as an experiment by the woman to test whether her jading recipe would work. But clearly, it appeared to be a form of magic to anyone not in the know.

At Mumby in Lincolnshire was a witch of whom a correspondent to *Lincolnshire Notes & Queries* recounted a story, telling how when a man she knew was driving his horses, "they would not pass her house, but went right up to her door, and wouldn't budge an inch till she came out" (*Lincolnshire Notes & Queries* series I, 1 70). At Longstanton in Cambridgeshire, the reputed witch Bet Cross is said to have stopped horses passing by on the road outside her garden (M. G. C. H. 1936, 507), and in the early twentieth century similar events were reported at Histon and Wisbech (Porter 1969, 57). Catherine Parsons records an incident in Horseheath, where a man was taking a load of corn to be malted, when the two black horses drawing his vehicle suddenly stopped. "Nothing could induce them to go on until the witch came out and patted them, and called them 'pretty dears,' then they quietly went on their way without further trouble" (Parsons 1915, 41). Miss Disbury of Willingham, active around 1900, was said to have the same power over cattle (Porter 1969, 175).

The famed Lincolnshire wise woman Mary Atkin was the wife of

a most respectable farm bailiff, who did not hold with her goings on, although he dared not check them. Several waggoners boarded in their house, and one morning, their breakfast bread and milk being sadly burnt, a lad threw his portion in her face. Quietly wiping it off she merely said, "Thou art very big now, my lad; but jest thou wait till thee and thy team gets to top of Cowbank: thou'lt be main sorry then, I'll go bail! See if thou ardn't." [Standard English: "You are very big now, my lad, but just you wait until you and your horses get to the top of Cowbank; you will be very sorry then, I swear. See if you are not."] All went well enough till they reached the place indicated, when suddenly the horses stopped short, shivered and sweated and shook, and not a step would they move one way or the other till, having called a man from a cottage near at hand, he went back and on bended knees besought Mary to lift the spell. When he returned the horses promptly moved on without further hitch. (Gutch and Peacock 1908, 73)

People in possession of the bone also have the power to stop animals. Enid Porter wrote of toadmen in Cambridgeshire, "They alone could make a horse move once they had ordered it, by word or by sign, to stand still. They were not unknown to exercise this power over horses of persons against whom they had a grudge" (Porter 1974, 31–32). A story is told at Bourn in Cambridgeshire about the blacksmith, George Kirk, who worked there in the early twentieth century and whose power came from his frog bone. One day, a local farmer offended all the men at the smithy by imputing them all of theft. He claimed that someone at the smithy had stolen some money intended for the payment of a bill. Kirk decided he would teach the angry farmer a lesson he would not forget. A little later, the farmer drove up to the forge in his pony trap. Kirk turned toward the road, took out his handkerchief, and held it to his nose, then put in back in his pocket. Kirk did no more, but when the farmer was ready to leave, his pony refused to start. Despite every effort on the farmer's part, the animal remained standing still where he had stopped it from nine o'clock in the morning until five o'clock in the afternoon. Then at five, George Kirk patted the pony's neck, and it went off as if nothing had happened (Davidson 1956, 69–70).

PERSECUTION

Occasionally, although the days of government-sponsored witch hunting had passed, its remnant, the Fraudulent Mediums Act, was used to prosecute astrologers and fortune-tellers and, in later years, spirit mediums. Scotch Jenny, a famed fortune-teller at Peakirk, near Peterborough, who died in 1798, was called a "wise woman" by the local press when she was prosecuted under this act and was forced to give up working publicly. In 1822, Lucy Barber of Market Deeping was brought to court and charged with obtaining money by foretelling the future. Upon returning the fee to her client and promising never to charge again, she was discharged.

The last trial in England for witchcraft took place at Hereford in 1712, in which Jane Wenham was convicted, but reprieved of the death sentence. In some places, the old fears of witchcraft surfaced occasionally and summary unofficial violence ensued. In 1808 at Great Paxton in Huntingdonshire, after Fanny Amey, an epileptic woman, in attempting to cross the frozen Great Ouse River, had fallen in and was seriously ill, a sixty-year-old woman called Ann Izzard was suspected of having used witchcraft to cause the accident and illness. In May of that year, a cart overturned close to Izzard in the St. Neots marketplace. That was taken as evidence she was a witch, and later a mob went to attack her house. In the night, they dragged her from her husband out of bed, beat her, and tore the flesh on her arms with pins. A local constable refused to assist her, and a neighbor who took her in was also later persecuted to the point where she gave up eating and died. Ann Izzard was attacked a second time and fled to live in another village. In 1809, the culprits were prosecuted and jailed, most of them for a month apiece (Saunders 1888, 156–64). At Sible Hedingham in Essex in August 1865, an eighty-year-old deaf-and-dumb French fortune-teller known as Old Dummy was accused of bewitching a neighbor. He was taken and thrown into a stream, where he was pelted with stones. Shortly afterward, he died (Howe 1952, 23–24). The culprits were arrested, convicted of manslaughter, and imprisoned. In Cambridgeshire in 1878, the funeral of the reputed witch Susan Cooper at Whittlesford was attended by large crowds, who expected strange manifestations to occur. After her interment, the children of the village school trampled on her filled-in grave "so that the imps couldn't get out" (Porter 1969, 175). The last recorded official accusation of bewitching among the rural population was after World War II at East Dereham (*News Chronicle* 1947). In the 1970s, at least one esoteric bookshop in England was firebombed by religious fanatics who objected to the books on witchcraft sold there. Intolerance and consequent violence is always just under the surface of society.

If we are to believe the testimony of a folklorist-clergyman, at least one wise woman believed the devil was coming to take her, the classic theme of one who has sold her soul. Writing in 1902, the Reverend R. M. Heanley recalled:

> It fell to my lot in 1885 to attend old Mary on her deathbed [Mary Atkin, the Lincolnshire wise woman]; in fact, she sent for me from another parish "to lay the Devil," whom she believed to have come for her. If nothing else had come, the hour of an evil conscience had undoubtedly arrived. She, at all events, firmly believed in her own powers, and, had it not been for the greater presence which she asserted was in the room, would, I fear, as little have regretted the use she had made of them. Her last words to me were: "Thou hast fixed him, Master Robert, for a bit, as firm as ivver I fixed anny; bud he'll hev' me sartain sewer when thou art gone." [Standard English: You have fixed him, Master Robert, for a while, as firm as I ever fixed anyone, but he will have me for certain, sure when you have gone."] And she died that night shrieking out that he had got her. (Heanley 1902, 13–17)

THE WILD HERB MEN

Connected with country practitioners and the horse doctors was a group of itinerant workers known as the wild herb men, who operated through Essex, Suffolk, Norfolk, Cambridgeshire, Huntingdonshire, and parts of Northamptonshire and Lincolnshire. They traveled around, digging for medicinal roots and herbs on remote patches of ground, deserted green roads, along hedgerows, railway cuttings and embankments, common land, the margins of orchards, and cliff tops (Hennels 1972, 79). The wild herb men claimed they had the right to dig in these places under an old charter, the Wild Herb Act, dating, they claimed, from Tudor times. The herb-digging season ran through the wintertime from November to April. The most sought-after herbs were dandelion and dock roots, for treating blood disorders; comfrey, used in treating sprains and open wounds; stinging nettle tops, made into an extract used to treat coughs and bronchitis; mandrake, for veterinary use only; horseradish, and couch grass roots, used in paper manufacture. They also unofficially dug roots of the "weird plants," used in country pharmacy, Horsemanry, and witchcraft. These included the roots of aconite, hellebore, monkshood, henbane, and the rare orchid whose bulbs, called "bull-bags," can engender love or hatred when used with skill (John Thorne, personal communication).

Root digging was profitable for the workers compared with ordinary farm laboring. A wild herb man could earn in one day the equivalent of a week's wages of an ordinary farm laborer. Even before the railways were built, wild herbs were transported long distances by regular carters' services, which offered cheap rates, because the herbs were medicinal and for the common good. Later the railway companies also offered competitive carriage rates for wild herbs. In 1972, the last master of the wild herb men, Cecil Grimes of Wisbech, recalled sending a consignment of wild herbs by the green herb rate by rail from Wisbech to Dunstable for two shillings, when an equivalent quantity of farm produce would have been charged five shillings (Hennels 1972, 80). The wild herb men stopped working in 1962 when the man who bought roots to process them went out of business. Thus, an old trade suddenly ceased, and with it much collective knowledge.

11

Geomantic Traditions and the Magic of Place

SPIRITS OF THE LAND: MAGIC IN PLACE

Throughout Europe, traditions and legends embody the principle that spiritual orderliness in human affairs comes from understanding that the land is ensouled. It has been taught since antiquity that a respectful, caring spiritual awareness of the land brings peace and plenty, a society based on goodwill, fecundity of herds and flocks, and a fruitful soil. Traditional relationships of people to the land are, of course, based on the activities of everyday life. Various climates and landscapes give each place its character, hunting and farming its rites and ceremonies, festivals, and gods. Everyone who lives close to Nature understands his or her oneness with the world.

There is a belief in the northern and western parts of East Anglia that each settlement has its own sprite guardians who come together to form a protective group called the Ward. The Ward sprites are benevolent beings who protect a village or town by night from both internal troubles and external dangers. At dusk each evening, the Ward sprites assemble at a particular place on the edge of the village, commonly a ward hill, and then travel by way of certain pathways to their watch places. Traditions from all over northern Europe tell that some paths are places where humans are unwelcome at certain times because spirits are traveling on them then. These paths can be reserved for the Good Ladies and the Princess of the Brilliant Star, who are considered fairies (called "fairises" in the eastern part of this region). Others are frequented by Gabriel Ratchets, Black Shuck, the Wild Hunt, or worse.

Some say that Ward sprites are guardian spirits of individual people in the settlement, both living and dead. The sprites' watch places are recognized stopping places in the landscape, the mounds, stones, shrines, crosses, and holy trees next to the roads and paths leading to and from the village. At night, if it has human acknowledgment and support, the Ward creates a protective spiritual ring around the settlement, providing protection against psychic attack from both the human and nonhuman realms. But each village's Ward is scarcely recognized anymore.

Individual benevolent sprites, not banded together to form the Ward, are hytersprites. Places where they reside feel good and friendly. Bad places in the landscape where humans intuitively feel psychically attacked are inhabited by malevolent yarthkins. These are earth spirits that express positive hostility to human interference. Unlike hytersprites, yarthkins cannot be placated with offerings presented to them in pleasing and beautiful ways. Such offerings merely serve to increase their bad intentions. As well as places with malevolent yarthkins, certain places have "invisible presences" that are not at all pleasant to encounter. Local lore describes each place by a particular name, though its nature is imprecise. In pagan times, places occupied by such harmful or hostile spirits were just left alone, but when the land began to be bought and sold as a valuable commodity, the old ways of reverencing places were not kept up. So in order to use such bad places effectively, techniques were devised that could block or nullify the baleful influence of yarthkins.

In East Anglia, the traditional arts of the cunning men who deal with such things employ sprite traps, blocking stones, staves, egg posts, and mirrors (Pennick [1995] 2004). The downside of the art of blocking and entrapment of spirits is that the precautions have to be reinforced periodically or the bad effects begin to appear again after a while. Where helpful sprites of the land are not acknowledged, or where they have been driven away deliberately, the land is spiritually dead. In East Anglia, this undesirable condition renders the land gast. In pagan Iceland, the word *álfreka* was used, and this is the common technical term in Britain used by practitioners today. It is clear that such places, no longer tended by their spiritual guardians, will inevitably become barren, and evil doings will happen there. This is the condition of many places today.

A state of sanctity exists when the innate spiritual nature of a place is manifested in visible, physical form; the ancient, traditional understanding of the divine is what has been described as organic religion.

Fig. 11.1. Nineteenth-century house in St. Ives, Cambridgeshire, with apotropaic sigils (*ing* runes) in brickwork.

The ancient ways of Europe acknowledge spirit guardians of fields and flocks: earth spirits; crop, tree, and water sprites; spiritual protectors of travelers and seafarers; supernatural beasts including trolls, water monsters, werewolves, phantom dogs, and dragons; personifications of disease and death; and demons who bring bad luck. Ancestral holy places—the homesteads, grave mounds, tombs, and battlefields—are venerated as places of ancestral spirits. These are the locations where people can experience transcendent states of timeless consciousness, receive spiritual inspiration, and accept healing. All of these manifest as the innate spiritual qualities of places that the Romans conveniently characterized as the genius loci, the spirit of the place.

The understanding of the nature of these spirits has varied from place to place and time to time. Until the arrival of Christianity in Europe, there was no philosophical barrier between the lofty beings of heaven and lesser earthly spiritual beings like dryads and land wights. The spiritual landscape was recognized as populated everywhere with spirits. The spirits of the earth were viewed as an integral part of a continuum in which the rocks and soil, plants and animals, wind and rain, and humans played their part as cocreators of life on Earth. Focused on local cults and shrines, this indigenous sanctity was overwhelmed by the incoming Christian religion, which looked to holy places on another continent as the focus of its devotions. Churchmen made a deliberate attempt to destroy this ancient understanding of the sacred landscape, labeling it heathen and viewing it as an enemy of their religion. In his laws known as the Dooms, Canute, King of Denmark and England from 1020 to 1023 CE, said, "Heathendom is . . . that they worship heathen gods, and the sun or moon, fire or rivers, water-wells or stones, or forest trees of any kind." Despite this and many other acts of persecution, many ancient beliefs and practices were not destroyed, but survive to this day in local tradition. Direct communion with the spiritual land is more powerful than any ancient text written by humans, even when it is believed to be divine.

The universal precepts of spirituality tell us that everything we do has a consequence, and so we should be aware of this. Geomantic traditions from the East and the West also tell us that when we alter the landscape we interfere with the natural flow of spirit, and unless we do something consciously and with proper knowledge, we will suffer unintended consequences. Knowledge of the techniques involved is used by individuals and groups to gain and exercise power over others. Magicians "putting the toad" on someone knew the precise places to bury the bones so that the cursed person would be most heavily afflicted. And the church has, since its inception, appropriated sacred locations and used places of power belonging to other spiritual systems. In 1972, the Bishop of Exeter in England issued a report titled *Exorcism.* It was the published opinion of a committee that had been convened by the Church of England's bishops, chaired by the noted Benedictine exorcist Dom Robert Petitpierre, and ecumenically included a leading Jesuit exorcist (Mortimer 1972).

Though it was hardly noticed outside churchly circles at the time of publication, it is a remarkable document with a bearing on practical geomancy and located magical practices. The report is a manual of exorcism of people and places, with an analysis and recommendations for the Anglican clergy. Of great interest are the bishop's committee's comments on place. They distinguished three kinds of forces that may be operating at any given place: those that are wholly human, those that are impersonal, and those that are demonic. They designated various kinds of place where "strain" can take place, that is, psychic disturbance of one kind or another. They are where souls of the departed (ghosts proper) are present, or where poltergeist, asportation, levitation, and other psychic phenomena occur. They can be places that hold memories, places that bear the psychic trace of some earlier personal action, or places that repeat an event in some way (Mortimer 1972, 21–22). These are rarely more than four hundred years old, we are told.

The Bishop of Exeter's committee claimed that some happenings were "haunts" deliberately instigated by magicians, and they said that a house or site used for "sexual misbehavior (in the countryside often the ancient fertility-cult site)" also generate these energies (Mortimer 1972, 21). They also determined that an office of an organization dedicated to greed or domination acts as a "dispersal center" for psychic disturbance (Mortimer 1972, 21). Finally, what the committee described as "Demonic Interference" is common on desecrated sites such as ruined sanctuaries: "This kind of activity and that of magicians frequently revivifies ancient Celtic sites such as tumuli, circles, and snake-path shrines, and so causes a general sense of 'buzz' or strain" (Mortimer 1972, 22). This report remains the major thinking on magic in the landscape in the Church of England.

In the European tradition are teachings about the *locus terribilis*. A locus terribilis is a place where human beings have never been welcome and ought never to trespass. These are the no-man's-lands recognized everywhere in former times (Pennick 2006a, 46). They are not intrinsically evil places, merely places where human presence is inappropriate. It is not very sensible to enter the crater of an active volcano; equally, to enter a locus terribilis is to court fatal peril. That is why one of their names is the Devil's Plantation (also the title of the grimoire owned by Daddy Witch at Horseheath). The unwary who enter such places are doomed: those who do so run a terrible danger by which, even should they escape alive, they will be forever marked. The spiritual nature of the locus terribilis is to ravage the human mind and body, not through revenge at the trespass, but as an impersonal and inexorable consequence of the human being there. Those who cross the line, who overstep the mark, have chosen to do so and will reap the results.

THE MAGIC CIRCLE

A tradition recorded in Norfolk and Cambridgeshire tells that the devil can be called up by making a circle on the ground while chanting a form of words. Thereby, an artificial locus terribilis is brought into existence. The circle is marked by flour, chalk, soot, salt, or sand. People discovering such a circle call it a "witch's circle." The circle, of course, is part of classic magic, protecting the magician inside from dangerous entities she or he may have evoked. Writing in 1915 about witchcraft in Horseheath, Catherine Parsons states that "a circle is drawn on the ground, with perhaps a piece of chalk . . . the Lord's Prayer is said backwards, and the devil suddenly appears within the circle, perhaps in the form of a cockerel, but all kinds of things are said to suddenly spring out of the ground" (Parsons 1915, 37). Parsons tells us also that "the devil usually appeared . . . in the form of an animal, such as a rat, mouse, or toad" (Parsons 1915, 32). "And if the person standing within the circle becomes so frightened that he steps out of the circle, we are told the devil would fly away with him" (Parsons 1915, 37). Sometimes the devil also appeared "in the likeness of a horse," black, of course, and took people on unwanted journeys. But a tradition from Lincolnshire tells us there is a way out, for even "if a person sells his soul to the devil, to be delivered at a certain specified time, the vendor, if wary, may avoid payment by putting in the contract 'be it in the house or out of the house' and then when the time arrives, sitting astride on a window sill or standing in a doorway."

Michael Clarke tells of a witch's circle found and photographed in the 1960s at Castle Acre in Norfolk. It was a soot circle, barely three feet in diameter, plainly made for a single individual. It was photographed before destruction. Finding such a circle has always caused fear and worry. If it is near a house, it may indicate that an on-lay has been created there. In 1615 at Haddenham, Cambridgeshire, Dorothy Pitman was tried for witchcraft and was asked "whether she had at any time made any circle, or did she know of the making of any circle by 'charmer, or enchantment,' to do any mischief?" (*Depositions and Informations,* F.10, Ely, 1615, cited by Parsons 1915, 38, 45). In western England, such circles are called gallitraps, a word also used for hedged-in pieces of land such as no-man's-lands (a.k.a. Clootie's croft and the Devil's Plantation). As magic circles, gallitraps are traditionally created by a "conjuring parson" to entrap criminals.

Traditions exist in various parts of Great Britain of making temporary patterns on the threshold or hearthstone. These threshold patterns and patterns chalked in dairies and stables are related to the magic circle tradition, though, as with all ornaments, their magical function is not specifically used to manage spirits, as is the circle. They are said generally to bring good luck and ward off harm. In Cambridgeshire, Foe-ing Out Day, the first of March, is the day for spring-cleaning, when the house should be swept and doorsteps should be scrubbed "to swill the winter fleas away" (Marshall 1967, 245). In Scotland, the West Country, Cheshire, and East Anglia, they may be drawn with chalk, pipe clay, or sand (Canney 1926, 13). Foe-ing Out Day in Cambridgeshire involves drawing threshold patterns on the doorstep in chalk. The local pattern, known only from Cambridge, is the Cambridge Box. In Newmarket and Cambridge, continuous patterns drawn around the floors of outhouses and stables are called the "running eight." These must be drawn in an unbroken movement, made without removing the hand during the process, the continuous looping patterns being made in a single sweep. These temporary floor patterns may be reflected by the permanent patterns found in floor-

Fig. 11.2. "Cambridge Box" threshold pattern in chalk traditionally drawn on Foe-ing Out Day, March 1, the day of spring-cleaning. The complex pattern is said to prevent the entrance of evil sprites into the house until the next Foe-ing Out Day.

ing made from bones, cobbles, bricks, and tiles. The patterns of East Anglian and Lincolnshire bit mats or rag rugs resemble those drawn on hearthstones and thresholds. Patterns often have a diamond in the center, a border, and triangles at the corner. Bit mats are made from material from worn-out old clothes cut into strips and attached to a fabric base using a pointed wooden tool called a "prooger."

Records from other parts of Britain hint at the function of different patterns. Ella Mary Leather records doorsteps in the Herefordshire villages of Dilwyn and Weobley having patterns made in chalk: "The stone would be neatly bordered with white when washed, with a row of crosses within the border" (Leather 1912, 53). In Shropshire, threshold patterns are created by rubbing bunches of elder or sometimes dock or oak leaves on the door or hearthstone. The color is said to last for weeks, even months. In Eaton-under-Heywood in Shropshire, patterns were "laid" on thresholds, stone steps leading to bedrooms, and the hearthstone. Here they are made "to stop the Devil coming down the chimney," exactly the function of the magic circle (Dakers 1991, 169–70).

12

Devilish Definitions

"HAVE YOU SEEN THE DEVIL?"

Those who dealt with hidden aspects of the material world, such as chemical substances, and those who dealt with the world of spirits came up against people in authority who had been taught to see the world through the biblical doctrines of the ancient Israelites. The wise women, witches, cunning men, and rural mystics dealt with things they felt and knew, things grounded in the seen and unseen worlds around them, emanating from the landscape in which they lived, rather than things they had been told by men who had read of them in books authorized by clerics. So all spiritual phenomena that clerics and enforcement officers encountered among the ordinary people were interpreted as manifestations of the primary biblical evil entity: the devil. The ancient Israelites had asserted that their national god was the only genuine one and the gods and goddesses of other tribes and nations were only concealed manifestations of the Israelites' antigod, the devil, so European followers of this theory centuries later believed that the beings and entities they called pagan were actually their devil in other forms.

The disastrous result was that, once the Christian religion had been imposed on England, those in authority invariably evaluated their contemporary human society in terms of the beliefs and teachings of ancient Israel, without regard to the entirely different circumstances of history, time, and place. The authorities' beliefs, imported from a totally different context, were incompatible with the traditional beliefs and practices of their subjects. The consequences of their attempts to impose the concepts and values of a different time, climate, and history on the common people of England were drastic, as the history of persecutions shows, crimes disguised as virtue.

The authorities made a serious category error when they claimed that every spiritual or magical act that was not performed by the Christian clergy was a manifestation of the Christian devil. This Judaeo-Christian terminology gradually filtered down from the elite into ordinary society, and those who practiced ancient traditional magical and sacred arts began to use the epithet the devil. In medieval times, the devil and his parallels were personated regularly during the performance of miracle plays and mystery plays performed by Christian religious orders and trade guides on the festal days of the calendar. In addition, there were

Fig. 12.1. Carving of the devil, painted red, on a seventeenth-century shop in Stonegate, York.

inns and taverns in several towns called the Devil. In London, next to the Devil Tavern, was the sign of the Black Dog, where in the 1680s the political agitator Abel Roper printed and distributed the majority of the pamphlets and songs that paved the way for the Revolution of 1688. He was the original printer of the famous song "Lillibulero."

When Roman Catholicism was abolished in England by King Henry VIII, the Protestants, returning again to ancient Israelite ideas, condemned these plays as idolatrous superstition. But as the costumes and props were valuable, unlike Catholic religious images, which were destroyed, the costumes of the mystery plays and miracle plays were put up for sale to anyone who would buy them. There is *A Boake of the Stuffe in the Cheyrche of Holbeach,* a record from 1543 that describes how the props of miracle plays were kept in the church at Holbeach until they were sold off (*Fenland Notes & Queries* I, 1889–1891, 64–65). So then the privatized properties and costumes of Catholic sacred plays were used in secular performances. Beelzebub, who appeared in many miracle plays, is an important character in many mummers' plays. In 1899, the Peterborough folklorist Charles Dack wrote, "Before Christmas, the Waits come round, and also the Morrice Dancers. These last are in the adjacent villages, and the old play is gone through. There is Belzebub, who comes in first, and says:

> *Here I come, Great Belzebub,*
> *Under my arm I carry my club;*
> *In my hand a dripping-pan,*
> *Don't you think I'm a jolly old man?*

There is the fight between King, or Saint George, and Beelzebub, in which King, or Saint George, is apparently killed, and the Doctor comes in and says:

DOCTOR: 'I'm the Doctor!'
BELZEBUB: 'What can you do?'

DOCTOR: 'I can cure pains within and pains without,
   Love-sick palsy and the Gout;
   And if the Devil's in I cast him out.'"

(DACK 1899, 16)

In the Plough Monday mummers' play at South Scarle in Nottinghamshire, the devil, or Beelzebub, is a man dressed in ordinary working clothes under an inverted sack with slits made in it for the head and arms. His whole body is padded thickly with straw and string run

Fig. 12.2. Beelzebub, a character in the Huntingdonshire mummers' play, performed by Northstow Mummers, Conington, Boxing Day, 1998. Photo by the late Rupert Pennick.

Fig. 12.3. Beelzebub, played by the author, with other members of the mummer's team, Lin Randall and Sally Tooley, Conington, Boxing Day, 1998. Photo by the late Rupert Pennick.

round the bottom of sack to keep it from falling out (Holmes 1952, 7). This links him with the Straw Men and Straw Bears of the Lincolnshire and Cambridgeshire Fens. In her *Fenland Chronicle,* Sybil Marshall recalled in 1967 that at Ramsey (where there was the best-documented Straw Bear) the molly dancers of the early twentieth century put on the traditional disguise and used devil masks (Marshall 1967, 84). A man sometimes personating the devil also appears as president of initiations in certain rural fraternities, such as the Horseman's Society and the Confraternity of the Plough. A Horseman's catechism from Scotland has the form of admittance for one who is already a member:

QUESTION: "Who told you to come here?"
ANSWER: "The Devil."
(*SOCIETY OF THE HORSEMAN'S GRIP AND WORD* 2009, 86)

At Aberdeen in the middle of the nineteenth century were published several editions of a book by William Singer called *An Exposition of the Miller and Horseman's Word, or the True System of Raising the Devil.* In it, Singer revealed the secret initiations of the Millers' fraternity and that of the Horseman's Society (Singer 1881). A man guising as the devil, otherwise called Auld Clootie, Auld Chiel, or Lucifer, is one of the officiants in revealed rituals of certain Scottish chapters of the Society of the Horseman's Word (see *Society of the Horseman's Grip and Word* 2009). Texts such as these must have influenced or enhanced the ritual, procedures, and teachings within other secret groups.

THE DEVIL MADE ME DO IT

The West Midlands cunning man Elijah Dunn was known as the Dudley Devil, and the particular initiation ceremonies, oaths, and rituals of several rural fraternities have a man who personates the devil. This figure, human or nonmaterial entity, is called the Deil, the Auld Gudeman, the Halyman, the Auld Chiel, and Auld Nick in Scotland;

the Black 'un in the West Midlands; Old Scratch and Old Ragusan in East Anglia; Nick, the Old 'un, the Old Lad, Samuel, Old Sam, Old Horny, Old Providence, and Bargus in the Fenlands; and Daddy in places as far apart as Devon and Cambridgeshire. The man personating this entity is present to empower the society's meetings and workings. It appears that the farther east one goes in East Anglia, the less likely the name the devil is used, but one of the nicknames; similarly, in the Lincolnshire part of the Fens, nicknames are used.

When the devil is personated in a rural fraternity's initiation ritual, the reported name is an epithet, not an actual name of power. Of course, he is invariably assumed by clergymen to be the Christian evil spirit called the devil, and thus the guildsmen were always misinterpreted as devil worshippers. The fear engendered even by the word *devil* meant that nonmembers made sure they kept well away from secret rites and ceremonies held at night in barns. As Gutch and Peacock recorded in 1908, "We were told, that the Lincolnshire folk never call the Devil openly by that familiar designation, but speak of him in an under-tone, as either 'Samuel,' 'Old Lad' or 'Bargus'" (Gutch and Peacock 1908, 65), for as the old adage tells us, "Speak of the devil and he will appear."

Daddy Witch was said to own a grimoire called *The Devil's Plantation*. The name of this book refers to the uncultivated corners of fields, deliberately left fallow by farmers because they are a no-man's-land, places where the spirits dwell. Inside the boundary of a no-man's-land, the pristine condition of the earth prior to its tilling by man is preserved. There, the land wights still have a place to be, and the prehuman wilderness is remembered. Uncultivated triangles of grass at the junction of roads are frequently actually called no-man's-land. Some of them still have stone crosses that may denote the Christianization of an eldritch holy place. They are well known in Scotland, where pieces of fenced ground, called the Halyman's Rig, the Gudeman's Croft, the Black Faulie, or Clootie's Croft, are places that neither spade nor plough is permitted to touch. Typically, they are the triangular corner of a field, fenced and dedicated by the farmer with a promise never to till the earth there (McNeill 1957, I, 62). The Devil's Plantation parallels the Scandinavian *stafgarðr,* "fenced enclosures" (Olsen 1966, 280). Early Christian legislation against pagan practices in England, Norway, and Sweden forbade people from worshipping at groves, stones, sanctuaries, and places designated stafgarðr: hence the connection in popular usage with the devil.

Horsemanry was the most important craft in premechanical days, and the skills to control horses were closely guarded secrets, taught only to initiates of three secret groups—the Horseman's Society, the Whisperers, and the toadmen. In 1949, the folklorist Enid Porter interviewed a retired horsekeeper in March, Cambridgeshire. He told her that a man who had performed the toad-bone ritual had to take the bone at midnight on three consecutive nights to the stables for his initiation to be functional (Porter 1969, 56). On the third night, the devil would appear and attempt to take the bone from the man. During the fight, blood would be drawn, and that event would make the man a fully initiated toadman, with the toadman's powers. It is said that as the devil attempted to wrest the bone from the toadman, he must keep it at all costs or lose his power and die. This very much appears as a man personating the devil conducting the initiation.

A story told by Eric Maple about Devil's House Farm on Wallasea Island near Canewdon, once the residence of Old Mother Redcap, tells how once a man entered the barn and felt overcome by an urge to hang himself. He put a rope around his neck, heard a voice saying, "Do it! Do it!" and saw a demon leering at him. But then he came to his senses, refused, and fled (Maple 1965, 220). The barn is always the place of initiation in rural fraternities, where the man personating the devil appears as the officiant. Mock hanging in the barn is part of the rite of the Horseman's Society in both Scotland and East Anglia. Perhaps the Devil's House Farm story is a garbled account of an initiation.

Arthur Randall, in his book *Sixty Years a Fenman,* recalled an incident with a Horseman on a farm near King's Lynn in 1911. One day, the Horseman asked the young man, "Have you ever seen the Devil, boy?" Arthur Randall answered that he had not, and hoped he never would. Then the Horseman replied, "Well I have, many a time, and what's more, I'll show you something." And he then demonstrated his power. He thrust a two-pronged fork into a dunghill and the horse was harnessed up to it. Then the horse was told to pull, but however hard it pulled, it could not draw the fork from the dunghill until the Horseman released it. After demonstrating his powers, the Horseman warned the young Randall, "Don't you tell nobody what you've just seen, boy" (Randall 1966, 109–10). Randall never recounted the event until after the Horseman had died. This is the classic prohibition of telling about the Nameless Art in this region, as in the story of Bet Cross. It is likely that the words "Have you ever seen the Devil?" are a Horsemen's fraternity recognition saying that Randall did not recognize and so failed to give the proper response. A Scottish Horsemen's admission saying that asks the Horseman who told him to come to the meeting is answered with "the Devil" (*Society of the Horseman's Grip and Word* 2009, 86). All secret fraternities have such questions that must be answered with a proper form of words that assures the questioner that one is an initiate. A wrong answer shows that he is not a member.

The devil was often called on in times of popular uprising against aristocratic oppression. The rebellion instigated in 1196 by William Fitzosbert, known as Longbeard, has an instance of this. As Frederick Ross recounts: "At this period the rich and the noble of the land were chiefly of the Norman race, and the poor almost all Saxons, who were ground down to the earth by the tyranny and oppression of their masters. . . . Richard Coeur de Lion was king, and had just been liberated from his captivity. He ruled the kingdom with a high hand, and had said on one occasion, when remonstrated with for raising money by unconstitutional means, 'Have I not a right to do what I like with my own? I would sell London itself if I could find a purchaser.' At this juncture up rose a lawyer, one William Fitzosbert, otherwise called Longbeard . . . he proclaimed himself the advocate of the poor, the redresser of their wrongs, and the unflinching enemy of their oppressors. Fitzosbert

Fig. 12.4. Traditional wooden grave marker, Barkway, Hertfordshire.

led a violent uprising in London, which eventually was defeated, and he and nine comrades were taken prisoner and condemned to death. "Longbeard was dragged by the heels to the Elms in Smithfield where he was hanged with nine of his comrades, where 'because his favourers came not to deliver him, he forsook Mary's son (as he termed Christ our Saviour), and called upon the Devil to help and deliver him. . . . The people, however, looked upon him as a martyr, secured his body, carried away the broken-up gibbet and the bloodstained earth as relics, and reports were afterwards spread abroad of sundry wonderful miracles which had been worked by their sacred influence" (Ross 1892, 41–43).

13

Magic, Farming, and the Land

THE LORE OF STRAW

Straw, the by-product of grain farming, has many uses. Straw rope or netting was used all along the western seaboard of Europe to tie down roof thatch. Thatch itself is often made of straw, though Norfolk reed is a material in East Anglia favored for its durability. Traditional beehives called "skeps" are made from straw rope wound spirally to form a dome, the ropes then being stitched together. Straw is also woven into hats, for which Luton is famed, and shoes, which have survived in temporary and ceremonial use (e.g., Evans 1965, 278; Bärtsch 1993, 59–82).

Straw is an important material symbolically. A Cambridgeshire courting custom uses a "true lover's knot" plaited from straw. The suitor gives his potential wife a straw plait, and if she wears it later pinned to her dress on the right side, it is a sign of rejection. If to the left, by the heart, with the ears of corn pointing right, it is a sign of acceptance (Porter 1969, 1–2). Under the feudal system introduced by the Norman Conquest, the signal for renouncing service was to break a straw (O'Neill 1895, 292). We say "to break faith" with someone and talks are "broken off," referring to the feudal straw. Another straw custom from feudal times is the brandon, a sign of legal seizure of the property of a dead vassal. Putting a stalk with a small wisp of straw dangling from its top is a traditional sign for stopping a path, and many tales of witches stopping horses tell of the straw in the road (O'Neill 1895, 292–93). The Yule straws traditionally burned at Aberdeen and other places are lightly twisted wisps of straw set alight and carried about in the dark, from whence comes one of the names for marsh lights, "will o' the wisp," which themselves are believed to be evil sprites. An exorcism of such an evil sprite recorded in the nineteenth century at Debenham, Suffolk, used a rushlight to lay a spirit that haunted a pond. "A clergyman he come with a rushlight, and put that in the pond, and he say the spirit were not to come out until the rushlight were burnt out. So he could never come out, for a rushlight could never burn out in a pond" (Mrs. H., quoted by Gurdon 1892, 558).

Traditionally, the last sheaf of the harvest has been taken triumphantly back to the community and honored. An account from Norfolk of the harvest on August 14, 1826, tells us "the last" or "horkey load" is decorated with flags and streamers, and sometimes a sort of kern baby is placed on the top at the front of the load. This is commonly called a "ben" (Hone 1827, II, 1166). One farming family in Huntingdonshire had a custom where the farmer carried the last sheaf home on his back (Tebbutt 1984, 72). "This nodding sheaf, the symbol of the god, also assumes animal shapes. In Lincoln, for instance, it is figured as an old sow or 'paiky'" (*Daily Chronicle*, September 12, 1904, quoted in Gutch and Peacock 1908, 210). The straw plait was made from the last sheaf; C. F. Tebbutt collected a straw plait from Alconbury, made around 1920 (Tebbutt 1984, 73). A visitor to the Cambridge Folk Museum in 1951 told the folklorist Enid Porter of a tradition from his grandmother's early years in Litlington, how the farmer held up the last shock of corn, and then one of the men made from it a figure—a proper dolly—with a head, arms, and legs. At the Horkey supper that followed the completion of the harvest, the figure was set in a special chair. Then, after the meal had finished, it was placed on top of the corner cupboard (Porter 1969, 123). Similarly, at Ramsey, the Straw Bear presided over the ploughboys' supper on Plough Monday. The placement in the corner reflects the continuing tradition of the Herrgottswinkel, or Holy Corner, in Scandinavia and Central and Eastern Europe and the uncultivated corner of the field, called the Clootie's Croft in Scotland and no-man's-land in Southumbria, which is likely to have been given the name the Devil's Plantation in Cambridgeshire (Pennick 2002, 99–101; Pennick 2003–2004, 139–40, 147).

There has been much written about the rites and ceremonies of the harvest, few of them participants' or eyewitness accounts, and there are many modern writings on how to make corn dollies that are heavily influenced by speculative writers who appear to have done little research into the matter. The name "corn dolly" is used now generically to describe any of the numerous forms of straw plaiting.

Fig. 13.1. Corn dolly in woman's form, Cartmel, Cumbria, 1995.

But the word *dolly* was not in general use until after World War II (as in the 1951 account above). The origin of the name "dolly" can be traced to a meeting of the Folklore Society in London on Wednesday, February 20, 1901, when "Mrs. Gomme exhibited and presented to the society a Kirn Maiden or Dolly, copied by Miss Swan from those made at Duns in Berwickshire" (Peacock 1901, 129). In a letter to Gomme, Miss Swan wrote, "I am sure that there was a good-luck superstition attached to the making and preserving of it, although it was not much talked about. The Kirn I sent you, though a modern dolly, is a faithful reproduction of those I have seen and helped to dress 'lang syne'" (Peacock 1901, 215–16).

The image exhibited to the folklorists was not a straw image made from the last sheaf for the harvest, but was a reproduction made as an example. Not being an actual kirn maiden used in harvest rites and ceremonies, it was called a dolly, just as a dolly represents but is not a real baby. An early reference, by William Hone on the Norfolk harvest ceremonies, remarks, "Sometimes a sort of kern baby is placed on the top at the front of the load" (Hone 1827, II, 1166). Papers and reports in the journal *Folk-Lore,* following Gomme's remarks on the subject and until World War II, call corn plaits by their actual names, for example, necks from Cornwall and Devon, and kern babies from Hereford and Long Crendon, Buckinghamshire. From the 1950s onward, the generic name "dolly" became the norm. By the 1960s, the new name had been analyzed etymologically by commentators as coming from *idol* (e.g., Evans 1965, 214; Butcher 1972, 463). No self-respecting participants in an actual Pagan tradition would call their sacred image an idol anyway, for this is a derogatory term for a non-Christian sacred image used exclusively disapprovingly by Christians. In addition, making straw images was now assumed to be a traditional woman's craft even though historical documentation showed otherwise.

The academic interpretation of pre- and para-Christian deities, demigods, and sprites as the Christian devil and his minions and the confusion generated thereby is seen in a record of the harvest in

Fig. 13.2. Corn lady illustration for the month of August by the author from *Göttinen in Mitteleuropa—Immerwährender Kalender,* Stuttgart, 2000.

Lincolnshire by a clergyman, R. M. Heanley, who nevertheless saw in the traditions relics of the Northern Tradition.

But no further back than last September [1899], I saw a veritable "kern baby" a largish doll cunningly twisted out of barley straw, and perched up on a sheaf exactly facing the gate of the grand wheat-field in which it stood. I missed seeing the owner, a small freeholder, but mentioning the matter to an old dame (of whom a Marshman would say, "them as knaws aal she knaws hezn't no need to go to no schule"). [Standard English: Those who know all she knows have no need to go to school.] She made a reply which proves that, what-ever else the Marshman has learnt of late to doubt, he still firmly believes in the Devil and his angels: "Yis, she be thear to fey away t' thoon'er an' lightnin' an' sich-loike. Prayers be good enuff ez fur as they goas, but t' Awmoighty mun be strange an' throng wi' soa much corn to look efter, an' in these here bad toimes we moan't fergit owd Providence. Happen, it's best to keep in wi' both parties." [Standard English: Yes, she is there to magic away thunder and lightning and suchlike. Prayers are good enough as they go, but the Almighty must have enough work to do to have so much corn to look after, and in these bad times we must not forget Old Providence. In that case, it's best to keep in with both parties.] (Heanley 1902, 12)

In 1951, the organizers of the Festival of Britain commissioned masters of the craft to create masterworks of the genre to celebrate the ancient craft. Old and new designs were put on show side by side; the Essex straw plaiter Fred Mizen made a straw lion and a unicorn (Cooper 1994, 62), while Arthur "Badsey" Davis, from a Worcestershire family that had handed down the craft through the male line made a crown-shaped plait from forty-nine straws, a design now known as Badsey's Fountain (Sandford 1983, 56). It is likely that this form originated as the crown of the rick (Lambert and Marx 1989, 88). Basket weavers, too, have made straw plaits when necessary. George Ewart Evans notes a man from North Essex who made corn dollies at Blaxhall, Suffolk. He did not put them on the last load, but they were used in the church as decoration during the time of the Harvest Festival (Evans 1965, 214). In recent years, a female corn dolly maker in Shropshire told me of a clergyman who refused to admit a straw plait to a church because he claimed corn dollies are pagan idols in complete ignorance of his own ecclesiastical tradition of harvest-time sheaves and straw plaits in church.

Straw plaits of many forms are made and offered for sale today. Some are taken from old traditions, and many new designs have arisen since the craft was disseminated widely in Britain after 1951 as a largely women's craft (unlike before) by the Women's Institute (see Croker 1971; Sandford 1983). Certain straw plait patterns or corn dollies are associated with this region. There are the Cambridgeshire Bell and the Cambridgeshire Umbrella (Butcher 1972, 464; Simper 1980, 112) and the Essex Turret or

Terret, the crown-piece ornament on a horse harness (Butcher 1972, 464). Butcher states that the bell recalls the Cambridgeshire custom of "ringing in the harvest" with handbells. Seahorses of straw are also particular to Essex, and the Suffolk Crown (Simper 1980, 114) is made along with the Suffolk Whip and Horseshoe (Butcher 1972, 464). Contemporary thatchers sometimes adorn house roofs with straw figures, most frequently pheasants and occasionally cockerels, though there are straw pigs on a house at Over, Cambridgeshire. In the twenty-first century, straw hares began to appear on newly thatched roofs in the Fens. Around the beginning of the twentieth century, Wright and Lones recorded straw rick ornaments in the region of Bedfordshire, Buckinghamshire, Cambridgeshire, and Hertfordshire that included ducks and foxes (Wright and Lones 1936, I, 188). In 1945, a number of corn stacks at Warboys and Fenton in Huntingdonshire were topped out with straw horseshoes, open at the top, in the center of the ridge, and *V*-shaped ones at each end, the letter *V* standing for victory, as World War II had just ended (Tebbutt 1984, 91).

In the collection at Roots of Norfolk at Gressenhall are a number of straw plaits that illustrate the historical diversity of dolly making through the twentieth century. The oldest is a straw plait that came from Essex, made in the nineteenth century from the final sheaf of the harvest and hung in the barn until the next harvest. There are three small corn dollies made by William Blake of Barton Turf, short bunches of wheat gathered and plaited; a plait in the form of a fisherman seated on a four-legged stool, made of wheat straw by Christine Palmer of Hilgay around 1967 when she was a pupil at Downham Market Girls' School; and two made in 1972 by a basket weaver, Walter Smalls of North Creake. These are plaits made to a pattern known as an American Clip Bond knot, for tying sheaves, and another made to a pattern called an Ordinary bond knot, depicting a tied sheaf (Frances Collinson, personal communication). The colors of the ribbons tied to corn dollies in this part of England have specific meanings: white for purity, red for the warmth of summer, green for fertility, blue for constancy and fidelity, and yellow for the ripe grain (Butcher 1972, 465).

The Old Sow is a little-known harvest tradition that appears to have been discontinued and not yet restored. "A lady who is a native of Lincolnshire tells me that in the first quarter of the present century [nineteenth] 'the old sow' used to appear in that county at harvest suppers." To the critical eye this curious animal was nothing more or less than two men dressed up in sacks to personate a traditional visitor to the feast. Its head was filled with cuttings from a furze bush, and its habit was to prick everyone whom it honored with its attentions. "I used to be very much afraid of it when I was a child," says my informant. "That was part of the harvest supper which I never could like" (*Notes & Queries* ix, no. 8, 128, quoted in Gutch and Peacock 1908, 209). It is significant that this name was given to a straw plait made in the same county, which links it with the animated straw man.

THE MAN OF STRAW

A man of straw has a different function from the corn baby or the rick ornament. He can be just an empty straw effigy, or may actually have a man inside. It is unnerving to see a seemingly lifeless straw man suddenly become animated. Unmanned straw men are a Lenten custom, sometimes burned at mid-Lent and there called Jack O'Lent. The German equivalent of Jack O'Lent appears on windowsills in southern Germany to this day during the period of Fastnacht (Shrovetide). Breughel's painting *The Battle of Carnival and Lent* (1559) has a clothed stuffed straw figure sitting on just such a ledge. Jack O'Lent is a straw man traditionally beaten, kicked, shot at, or burned. In Cornwall, he is identified with Judas Iscariot (Wright and Lones 1936, I, 38).

Straw effigies of Judas are burned of Good Friday in Liverpool, and a German tradition has the same figure, which used to be called Ostermann—the Wandering Jew. In Germany, this straw man is alternatively called the Todpuppe—a symbol of death that is used in the rite of

Fig. 13.3. The older form of the Straw Bear at Whittlesey, prior to the police ban in the early twentieth century. Drawing by the author.

Todaustragen, "driving out death" (Flaherty 1992, 40–55). In his 1863 book, *Das Festliche Jahr,* Freiherr von Rheinsberg-Düringsfeld wrote that the effigy of Death was "made of old straw. Sticks serve him as his arms and legs, the face is old white linen, the head is covered with an old cap or wound around with a white cloth and the body is clad in old clothing. When the figure is thus dressed, the young people dance hand-in-hand around it, singing and jeering . . . at last they drag Death to the bridge and from there throw him into the water beneath, or they take him to a cliff and throw him down." There is a Guernsey tradition to make a straw man on New Year's Eve, *le vieux bout de l'an,* representing the old year, then take him with a torchlight procession to the beach, where he is burned. The Bonfire Night custom in Kirton-in-Lindsey, Lincolnshire, used not an effigy of Guy Fawkes, but a straw man (Peacock 1907, 450).

I have already mentioned a straw bear in connection with Plough Monday at Ramsey. In addition to making small figures of straw to commemorate a successful harvest or to crown a hay rick, there is an eastern English custom of dressing a man in straw. Scarecrows are traditionally made from old clothes stuffed with straw, and the plough jags, or plays, of Burringham in Lincolnshire have a character called Joe Straw, his clothes stuffed with straw and with a goose feather in his hat (Wright and Lones 1938, II, 94). A late nineteenth-century account of Plough Monday at Wichford, near Ely, tells us, "In the eve of the second Monday of January, several young men form a party. They go together and get someone to lend them a plough and some whips; and then they get some straw and put it on their backs; and then they black their faces" (Frazer 1897, 184). Belts and *lalligags* of woven straw were worn at Brandon Creek on Plough Monday, and at Littleport, Humpty, the Broom Man, wore a tail made of braided straw (Porter 1969, 101–102).

In 1933, Ethel Rudkin reported an account of the Straw Man at Holton-le-Clay in Lincolnshire. Here the Straw Man appeared on Plough Monday in the plough jags.

> Many's and many's the time I'se been round wi' the Plough Jags. I can't remember the play as we used to do, but Straw Man was the first speaker I remember. Carry this 'ere Straw Man for *miles*, we did—carried 'im right way into a house, an' set 'im down, tail an' all, an' as soon as 'e was set down 'e made a long speech, after which the play began. Straw Man 'ad to be a big man, 'an 'e was all covered with straw, an' a great long straw tail that hung down an' trailed behind 'im. We never took a plough with us, but allus took Straw Man. (Rudkin 1933, 282)

The connected custom of parading a straw-clad man called a Straw Bear through the streets is recorded from Whittlesea (sometimes also spelled Whittlesey) and Ramsey. The Ramsey Straw Bear is mentioned in connection with Plough Monday in the *Peterborough Advertiser* for January 16, 1886, written with typical Victorian-class disapproval, "The day was observed here by the customary exhibition of blackened faces, and not over modest petitions for 'just one,' emphasized with ingenious clattering instruments of torture, and promoted with much clamorous importunity. The 'Straw Bear' also favored us with a visit, capering to the dulcet accompaniment of the concertina, and showing his affinity to the shaggy creature impersonated by an ursine grunt of satisfaction for a small contribution" (*Peterborough Advertiser* 1886). A correspondent to *Fenland Notes & Queries* records how "the custom on Straw Bear Tuesday was for one of the confraternity of the plough to dress up with straw one of their number as a bear and call him the Straw Bear. He was then taken round the village to entertain by his frantic and clumsy gestures the good folk who on the previous day had subscribed to the rustics' spread of beer, tobacco, and beef, at which the bear presided" (*Fenland Notes & Queries,* IV, 1899, 228).

The closeness of this Plough Monday/Tuesday tradition with the straw man in the northern part of the region has been ignored because of the difference in names, man, and bear. Straw Bear Tuesday is the day following Plough Monday (Wright and Lones 1938, II, 103–4). "On the day following Plough Monday," F. W. Bird tells us in his 1911 memoirs, "There was Straw Bower Day, when those who had been witches paraded the town clad from head to foot in straw, and in that guise solicited tolls and alms. But this custom did not prevail in Godmanchester" (Bird 1911, 40). It is possible that the name Straw Bower was altered into Straw Bear, whereas farther north, the figure remained a straw man, appearing also in ran-tanning and on Guy Fawkes Night. In her *Fenland Chronicle,* Sybil Marshall made the claim that the Ramsey Straw Bear was a custom that used to belong to another day, but got mixed up with plough witching at some time by chance. The bear was led at night on a chain from pub to pub and house to house. As with the Holton-le-Clay straw man, the bear appears to have been associated with a mummers' play, which unfortunately appears to be unrecorded (Marshall 1967, 200–201). Plough Monday celebrations at Ramsey were reported in 1927, but records of the bears' outings are scanty (*Peterborough Advertiser* 1927).

In Whittlesea, the custom was actively suppressed in 1907 by police action, though in the 1970s, I was told by an old Whittlesea woman that a Straw Bear was made on later occasions, even after World War I, and went clandestinely from house to house between police patrols. It is likely that the police destroyed the custom at Ramsey, too, and in other places where it may not be recorded. In a memoir written on January 12, 1909, G. C. Moore Smith reported, "I was told that two years ago a zealous inspector of police had forbidden 'Straw Bears' as a form of cadging, and my informant said that in many places they had been stopped by police. He also said that at Whittlesey the police had prevented the people on Plough Monday from taking round the plough" (Frazer and Moore Smith 1909, 202–3). In 1976, the folk-rock musician Ashley Hutchings issued a record titled *Rattlebone and Ploughjack,* on which the whole of Moore Smith's memoir was read out, to the accompaniment of a tune Hutchings had recorded of George Green playing on the melodeon. Green, who was a molly dance musician in the 1930s and was famed for his off-the-wall

Fig. 13.4. The Straw Bear at Whittlesea, 2006.

version of "The Cambridge Hornpipe," remembered the tune as that played for the Straw Bear, thereby preserving it from oblivion. *Rattlebone and Ploughjack* led to the reinstatement of the Straw Bear in 1980 as an annual event. The appearance of the Straw Bear led to the present annual Straw Bear Festival, which, however, is held on a Saturday and not the customary Tuesday after Plough Monday.

When the custom was brought back at Whittlesea, the design of the bear was altered, the new one following German custom with a sheaf over the head as at Jena and Wilflingen (Frazer 1931, 87; Pennick 2006b, 95). Two photographs from lantern slides, one taken in the street and the other a posed studio photograph, were made some time before 1909. In 1909, these lantern slides belonged to the local schoolmaster, Henry Slater. They both show the Straw Bear with a quite different appearance to that of today, indistinguishable from the straw man of nearby Lincolnshire.

The post-1980 Whittlesea Straw Bear Festival has become a big event, with performers traveling from all parts of England and even

Fig. 13.5. The Straw Bear at Wilflingen, Germany, 1999.

a German straw bear gang from Walldürrn appearing regularly. In some years, a special ale has been brewed and special sausages made. In recent years, however, actions taken by the organizers, the local council, and the police have again curtailed the event, reducing the range of the bear's parade and removing much of its traditional spontaneity. At Whittlesea, the straw bear (minus a man inside) is burned on the following Sunday. In the early years of the reinstatement, pieces of part-burned straw were recovered from the fire and taken away as souvenirs or good-luck charms, though in later years the fire has been fenced off and spectators kept away from it in typical modern "health and safety" fashion. In 2009, the Ramsey Straw Bear was reinstated, with local school children performing molly dances and a version of the Cambridgeshire broom dance.

The straw man was not only a Plough Monday and Tuesday custom in the Fenlands and their purlieus. He also was brought out for rantanning. This tradition is recorded from several Lincolnshire villages, including Langwith, Willoughton, Winterton, and Holton-le-Clay, where the straw man also appeared on Plough Monday. "If any man had offended the community, by behaving badly to his wife, beating her etc.," he would be given a warning to stop, but if he continued, "then the people took the law into their own hands," and the person was rantanned. In 1933, an incident was recalled by a Mr. L. from Holton-le-Clay where a schoolmaster beat a boy severely and left him tied by his thumbs to a clothesline. Even by the rough and brutal teaching standards accepted as normal then, this treatment "so enraged the villagers that they went and Rantanned him."

The locals got kettles and cans and borrowed a piece of sheet iron from the blacksmith. Two people held the sheet, and several others beat it with sticks and hammers. The ran-tanners went to the schoolmaster's house with the straw man in the lead. They ran-tanned the schoolmaster for three successive nights: "We allus Rantanned for three nights like that because there was 'no law.' The third night when we's sung songs an' made a big din outside 's 'ouse for a long time, we all went to the bit of a green there was outside the public 'ouse, an' we burnt the straw man—only the straw offen the man, you know, but we called it 'Burnin' the Straw Man'" (Rudkin 1933, 292).

A ran-tanning song from Willoughton threatened to put a wife beater "in the news," that is, the obituary column.

> *Ran tan tan!*
> *The sound of an old tin can.*
> *He did lick her,*
> *He did kick her,*
> *He gave her a sad bruise,*
> *And if he does the likes again,*
> *We'll put him in the News.*

Usually, the ran-tanned man stayed indoors and dared not show himself. Many who "got out of the house" were beaned, that is, beaten with short-stocked whips with five thongs, then thrown in the pond. The straw man presided at the punishment (Rudkin 1933, 292–93).

Although a prominent politician of the late twentieth and early twenty-first centuries is called Jack Straw, the most famous Jack Straw was one of the leaders of the peasants' revolt of 1381. The connection of straw with rebellion is known from thirteenth-century France, where the rebel Paillers carried about a bottle of straw called a *paille,* with which they burned the property of their oppressors (O'Neill 1895, 296). It is likely that Jack Straw's name comes from the connection of the straw man with rebel incendiarism. He was a well-known figure in the folk tradition, and a play from 1593, *The Life and Death of Jack Straw, a Notable Rebel in England,* recounts his struggles against the royal tax collectors, taking the cause of the poor and disposed against the rich overlords. "Neighbors, neighbors . . . but marke my words, and follow the counsell of John Ball, England is gone to such a past of late, that rich men triumph to see the poore beg at their gate." Of course, the rebel Jack Straw was killed in 1381, but his example lived on. He appeared as a character in mummers' plays and was banned by an ordinance of King Henry VIII in 1517, "that Jack Straw and all his adherents should be henceforth utterly banisht, and no more be used in this house." Jack Straw also is a character in a number of mummers' plays from Ireland (Gailey 1974, 1–22).

With my whim wham whaddle O!
Jack Straw straddle O!
Pretty boy bubble O!
Under a broom.

14

Tools of the Craft

BROOMSTICK, FLAIL, AND CROOMSTICK

Although the besom is stereotypically the witch's broomstick, the besom was the traditional broom used by everyone before it was largely ousted by factory-made brooms. In this region, the stale, or handle, is traditionally made from ash wood, and the broom part from twigs of

Fig. 14.1. Comberton broom dancer, the late Cyril Papworth, dancing on Plough Monday, 1997. Drawing by the author.

birch, hazel, rowan, or a mixture of them. The twigs are bound to the stale by withies made of willow. Brooms are customarily only made at certain times of year. It is unlucky to make a new broom during the Twelve Days of Christmas or in the merry month of May. Brooms have a significance that goes beyond mere sweeping, though sweeping in itself has a magical dimension. It is an East Anglian custom for a man to hang out a broom when his wife is away, so that his friends can come and drink with him, or other women can visit him.

In 1933, Dr. Charles Lucas of Burwell recalled how his father had seen brooms sticking out of the windows of a wine merchant's shop in Swaffham Bulbeck, and inside was a large group of men drinking wine (Porter 1969, 391). The same tradition, called Besenwirtschaft, is customary in southern Germany, where people are invited by the displayed broom to come into the farmhouse to drink wine. Prudence Jones recounts that when she was there in 1978, the Green Man public house in Gosfield displayed the broomstick when the landlady was absent (Jones 1979, 9). A common interpretation of hanging out the broomstick is that it is an invitation by the man of the house to women to visit him when his wife is absent. The broom is used in customary handfastings, where, hand-in-hand, the couple jump over the broomstick to announce that they are formally together.

The Broom Man is part of the molly dance gang, and in some mummers' plays, Little Devil Doubt carries a broom with which he mock-menaces the audience and demands money. Although he guises as a devil, Little Devil Doubt actually sweeps evil spirits (devils) out of houses in New Year rites, *doubt* meaning "do-out." Generally, a factory-made broom is used by contemporary Little Devils Doubt. In molly dancing and mumming, the broom is a practical tool, used in wintertime to sweep away snow. It is also used in the broom dance that sometimes accompanies mummers' plays.

In the days before the mechanization of farming, threshing the grain was done by hand using a flail. The flail, known as the stick-and-a-half, is made from a stick (handle) of ash and blackthorn or holly wood for the upper part, the swingle (Evans 1965, 93). The swingle is attached to the handle by thongs of eelskin or snakeskin. An East Anglian saying, "There is no fence against the flail," means that one cannot ward off blows when a flail is used against one as a weapon; figuratively, "You cannot guard against the attacks of a person who utters blunt, unwelcome truths without any restraint from good manners" (Forby 1830, II, 428). The flail is an effective weapon when used at close quarters. William Hogarth's 1758 print *The Election: Chairing the Members* shows a man armed with a cudgel fighting a man armed with a flail. A different kind of flail, neither used for threshing nor thrashing opponents, is the sprite flail. This is a magical tool used to clear pathways that are known to be infested with sprites or ghosts, or paths that have not been walked for a time and need reopening magically as well as physically. It is made from nine thorny bramble branches, each an ell (26.5 inches) in length, tied together with willow bark. The sprite flail should be swished from side to side like a whip or broom in a sweeping action as the user walks slowly forward along the sprite-infested path.

A croomstick is a stick with a curved end. There are various versions: shepherds' crooks and cleeks, market sticks, dipping hooks, scrumping sticks, and croomsticks for viewing the sky. A traditional way of making one is to pin down a growing sapling of appropriate size to the ground so that the stem bends naturally to upright itself. This is a process that takes several years and produces a bend quite different from those made by stick makers who steam-bend their wood. Croomsticks are useful in getting things "by hook or by crook."

RHABDOMANTIC RODS

Water divining or dowsing with a hazel rod used to be a common craft in the countryside. Its origin is uncertain, but it appears to date from the seventeenth-century magical texts on rhabdomancy. Although it became a purely practical art with little surrounding ritual, in its early form it was certainly a magical technique. It appears to have reached the country practitioners from ceremonial magicians. According to the dowsing historian Colonel Bell, 1638 is the earliest known reference to dowsing in England. It appears in Robert Fludd's *Philosophia Moysiaca* (Bell 1965, 2). George Day ascribes the spread of the art of dowsing to Pierre Thouvenel in France in the eighteenth century and in England to Mr. Cookworthy of Plymouth (Day 1894, 81). Clearly, dowsing is a form of magic, not science, as later practitioners claimed.

Day quotes *The Shepherd's Kalendar or the Citizen's and Countryman's Companion* of 1706, which gives instructions how to make a "Mosaic wand to find hid treasure." One must "cut a hazel wand forked at the upper end like a Y. Peel off the rind and dry it in a moderate heat; then steep it in the juice of wake-robin or night-shade, and cut the single lower end sharp, and where you suppose any rich mine or treasure is near, place a piece of same metal you conceive is hid in the earth to the top of one of the forks by a hair or very fine silk or thread. . . . At the going down of the sun, the moon being on the increase . . ." (Day 1894, 81–82). Day tells us that among the many virtues ascribed to the rod is that of detecting underground water or veins of minerals: "The rod is a little forked stick of hazel or some other wood. The operator takes one of the branches in each hand, and, extending the shaft or stem horizontally from his body, moves slowly over the spot that is supposed to conceal the spring of water or the vein of coal" (Day 1894, 82–83).

Water divining appears to have been uncommon in the late nineteenth century, and there seem to be no particular recorded local traditions from that time. The British Army, however, was a significant element in the transmission of dowsing to wider society, and the history of British dowsing is filled with the names of high-ranking military officers. Water divining was of use in overseas military campaigns where sources of water had to be found for camping troops. But the most famed rhabdomant of the late nineteenth century was not a professional soldier. He was John Mullens, who came from Chippenham in Wiltshire. He was known as the Man with the Twig, using a blackthorn rod, not a hazel one (Day 1894, 83). In 1874, the local press in Grantham, Lincolnshire, noted that Mullens was dowsing there, and Day notes that Mr. Christy Miller of Broomfield in Essex called in Mullens in June 1891 to seek water. So it appears there were few practitioners of water divining at the period, and no specifically local traditions are certain. A. K. Barlow of Braintree was dowsing for water in September of that year, but who taught him is uncertain. Day records a notice in the daily press in December 1893 that "a good spring of water has just been found at Thremhall priory . . . by means of a divining rod" (Day 1894, 80). Subsequent dowsing in this region has followed national and international practices and fashions, and there are no specifically local traditions.

BLOODSTONES

Bloodstones are the traditional remedy to stop a cut from bleeding. The number 9 is significant in the workings of the bloodstone. One is hung on a red silk ribbon around the person's neck. It is tied with three knots three inches apart. To activate a bloodstone for a man, nine drops of a woman's blood must be dripped onto it, and for a woman, nine drops of a man's blood. Bloodstones themselves are not actually stones, but special blood-red glass beads. A bloodstone in the author's possession comes from King's Lynn, perhaps made by a nineteenth-century Frenchman who produced them in King's Lynn. A bloodstone seen by a folklorist in 1911 was made of dark-green glass containing white and orange twists (Porter 1969, 83). In 1865, George Rayson noted an East Anglian remedy against nosebleeds, which was to wear a skein of scarlet silk around the neck, tied with nine knots down the front. The knots should be tied by a man for a woman, and vice versa. But Rayson made no mention of the bloodstone (Rayson 1865c, 217).

LUCK STONES

Holeystones or hag stones are flints with a natural hole right through them. They are considered lucky, warding off the ministrations of harmful sprites. They should be hung by a string or wire on the back of the door in stables to keep the horses calm at night (Glyde 2008, 179; Evans 1971, 181–82) and over beds to prevent nightmares. Sometimes holeystones taken from the beach are threaded together into chains for extra efficacy. Holed flints were used by the noted Arts and Crafts Movement architect and Cambridge professor Edward Schroeder Prior at strategic points on the exterior walls of Henry Martyn Hall in Cambridge, following local tradition (Pennick 2006b, 96). Another magical stone in this region is the fossil called variously fairy loaf, frairy loaf, or pharisee loaf. This is a fossil echinoderm whose shape resembles

Fig. 14.2. Chain of holystones, Great Yarmouth, Norfolk.

the traditional loaf of baked bread. Fairy loaves should be kept polished and left on the main room's mantelpiece or the kitchen windowsill. For as long as a fairy loaf remains there, the explanation goes, there will always be bread in the house. In other contexts, these stones are called shepherd's crowns (Evans 1971, 129–30).

BREEDING STONES

The conglomerate stones formed of glacial gravel and pebbles cemented together naturally have a striking appearance, unlike any other stone. Customary names for this notable stone are breeding stone, growing stone, *oculatus lapis,* and mother stone. In parts of Essex, they are called breeding stones because they are said to be the source of all small stones found in fields (Griffinhoofe 1894, 144). In 1881, J. W. Saville of Dunmow noted, "So far as Essex is concerned, not only the name but the fact implied is implicitly believed in, and that small stones increase in size and number" (*Notes & Queries,* 6th series, IV, 1881, 478). Known in Hertfordshire as plum-pudding stones, they are much prized as lucky amulets, being placed in prominent locations (Jones-Baker 1977, 95, 190).

WITCH BOTTLES AND SPRITE TRAPS

This region has many examples of an apotropaic device that has a recorded magical function and theory behind it: the witch bottle. In 1908, Gutch and Peacock reported a find of one in Lincolnshire.

A few years ago, in pulling down an old house in a neighbouring village [probably Messingham], a wide-mouthed bottle was found under the foundation, containing the heart of some small animal (it was conjectured a hare), pierced as closely as possible with pins. The elders said it had been put there to "withstand witching." Sometime after, a man digging in his garden in the village of Yaddlethorpe came upon the skeleton of a horse or ox, buried about three feet beneath the surface, and near to it two bottles containing pins, needles, human hair, and a stinking fluid, probably urine. The bottles, pins, etc., came into my possession. There was nothing to indicate the date of their interment except one of the bottles, which was of the kind employed to contain Daffy's elixir, a once popular patent medicine. The other bottle was an ordinary wine pint. At the time when these things were found, I mentioned the circumstance to many persons among our peasantry; they all said that it had "summut to do with witching" and many of them had long stories to tell, setting forth how pins and needles are a protection against the malice of the servants of Satan. (Gutch and Peacock 1908, 96)

There is contemporary documentation from the time when witch bottles were in use. In 1681, Joseph Glanvil wrote about them in *Sadducismus Triumphatus, or Full and Plain Evidence Concerning Witches and Apparitions* (published 1689). Glanvil tells of William

Fig. 14.3. Magic bottles, some sealed and containing tangled threads, trapping sprites.

Brearly, a priest who was a fellow of Christ's College, Cambridge. He took lodgings in a Suffolk village where strange occurrences took place. His landlady appears to have suffered ill health for some time, which was blamed on a phantom "thing in the shape of a bird." The phantom was reported to "an old man who traveled up and down the country." He recommended that the landlady's husband should "take a bottle and put his wife's urine into it, together with pins and needles and nails, and cork them up, and set the bottle to the fire, but be sure the cork be fast in it, and that it not fly out." The husband followed the prescription, but the cork blew out. A second successful attempt followed, and "his wife began to mend sensibly, and in competent time was well recovered. But there came a woman from a town some miles off to their house with a lamentable outcry, that they had killed her husband. . . . At last they understood that her husband was a Wizard and had bewitched this man's wife, and that this counterpractise prescribed by the Old Man, which saved the man's wife from languishment, was the death of the Wizard that had bewitched her" (Glanvil 1689).

The commonest witch bottle discovered in buildings and beneath thresholds is called a greybeard or a bellarmine, the latter name being from an alleged likeness to Cardinal Bellarmine (1524–1621), a Roman Catholic inquisitor and persecutor of Protestants in the Netherlands when that land was ruled by Spain. However, it is not until 1634 that we find the first record of the name Bellarmine, in *The Armory*, a play by William Cartwrict. In addition, these bottle jugs were being made for a generation before the notorious cardinal ran the Spanish Inquisition in Holland. They were made in the Rhineland from around 1500 and shipped across to England. Manufacture ceased around the beginning of the eighteenth century. Bellarmine bottles are squat, round-bellied stoneware vessels, commonly five to nine inches in height, with a brown salt-glazed surface. On the front they are imprinted with a bearded face on the neck and a coat-of-arms or another sigil beneath it. The name was officially recognized academically in 1849, when a paper about them using the name was read by William Chaffers before the British

Archaeological Association. When Chaffers was talking about them to learned clergymen and academics, they were still in use by country cunning men.

Witch bottles containing the materials described by Glanvil have been unearthed in many places in southern England, and those from this region are on view in museums in Bury St. Edmunds, Cambridge, St. Ives, and Wisbech. Those whose contents have been scientifically analyzed show that they contained pins or nails and urine in addition to other organic materials (e.g., Bunn 1982, 5; Massey 1999, 34–36). One found in Ipswich contained a heart-shaped piece of felt, stuck with pins. Ralph Merrifield considered that the witch bottle was first introduced into East Anglia, from whence it spread to other regions of England (Merrifield 1954; Smedley 1955, 229). Reported witch bottles from old inns appear to be frequent, perhaps because the constant passage of customers necessitated additional magical protection, enhardening the inn against harmful magic and psychic disturbance. The foundation rituals for inns, if there was any coherent body of tradition, may have included

Fig. 14.4. Magical artifacts found in the fabric of buildings in Cambridgeshire, including two Cambridgeshire witch bottles and a ceramic model church found up a chimney in Histon.

special rites requiring witch bottles. These traditions, if they existed, are now lost to us (Pennick 1986, 18).

The use of nails and the heart-shaped piece of felt found in an Ipswich witch bottle link it with nail magic. Various charms of this kind have been discovered in chimneys of old houses all over England. In 1892, a bullock's heart pierced with nails and thorns was discovered in a chimney of a house at Shutes Hill Farm at Chipstable in Somerset. With it was "an object, said to be a toad, also stuck with thorns" (Ettinger 1943, 246). The function of this kind of magic was described by a writer in the *Times* in 1917, who noted, "A sheep's heart pierced with pins and nails to break the spell of a black witch . . . was prepared by an old woman who practised in London as late as 1908" (*Times* 1917). It was hung in the chimney to accomplish its task.

In addition to Bellarmines, the Cambridgeshire witch bottle is a common form. Much smaller than their stoneware counterparts, they are made of clear glass with a green or blue tinge. The locus for the Cambridgeshire witch bottle is predominantly in the wall above the

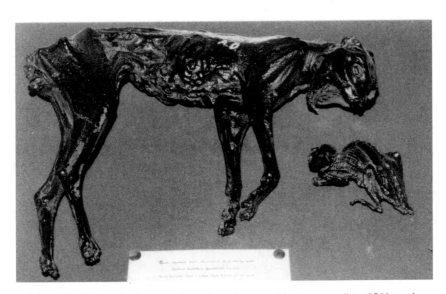

Fig. 14.5. Mummified cat and rat found embedded in a wall in 1811 in the former W. Eaden Lilley department store, Cambridge, and kept in the director's office until its closure in the 1980s.

Fig. 14.6. East Anglian sprite trap, used to entangle troublesome sprites. Once a sprite is caught, the thread is removed and tangled up. Then it is put in a bottle, which is then sealed, permanently trapping the sprite. Drawing by the author.

lintel of a door. These witch bottles are long and narrow, occasionally slightly conical like that in the Wisbech museum. They contain strands of colored thread, with red (the "witch color") predominant (Pennick 1986, 18). Black horsehair has been found in at least one case. The threads may come from a sprite trap, set up to entrap harmful sprites, yarthkins, ghosts of the unquiet dead, and discarnate entities. Sprite traps are made from a stave of blackthorn, at the top of which is attached a loop of copper wire. A smaller loop of copper wire is also made, above which a small metal *Dag* sign, the runic character *D,* is fixed, linking the inner ring with the outer. The red thread is wound around the loops, rather in the manner of a bicycle wheel. The metal parts are bound to the blackthorn stick with red thread.

The sprite trap is put together at sunrise with a ceremony that empowers the trap to capture the harmful sprite or entity. It is set up at night on a path known to be affected by the harmful sprite, ghost, or yarthkin, the sort of place one would use a sprite flail when walking, such as a bier balk or coffin path near a graveyard (Pennick [1995] 2004, 130). After an appropriate time, the trap is examined to see whether the offending sprite has been entangled in it. If the test proves

Fig. 14.7. The date 1946 is visible in bottle ends on the last timber-frame building built in Norwich after the massive destruction of large parts of the city by aerial bombardment during World War II. It was traditional to embed bottles containing magical objects in the walls of new buildings.

positive, the trap is taken away to a consecrated circle where the threads are removed and sealed in a bottle to imprison the sprite. The thread is cut from the trap using a consecrated knife, and the pieces are put into a previously consecrated Cambridgeshire witch bottle with the following spell recited:

> *Thread, tie up this sprite,*
> *Free us from its spite,*
> *Tangle up the bane,*
> *Let not a jiece* remain.*
> *Ka!*

The bottle is closed immediately with a cork, tied with new red thread (not the thread from the sprite trap), and sealed over with red

---

*A *jiece* is the smallest piece of anything.

wax. Should the seal ever be broken, then the sprite will be liberated and wreak havoc on the person who opened it. The bottle is then buried in a wall, where it serves to ward off other sprites, ghosts, entities, and general ill wishes (Pennick [1995] 2004, 105–106).

These and many other magical techniques were the commonplace of people living and working in the rural society of this region in the past. They are not exceptional; they were the norm. The magical view of the world, dismissed as superstition by the predominant modern worldview, was a valid means of living under harsh and difficult circumstances, and it enabled our ancestors to survive and even flourish when good years brought good harvests. There is much that can be learned from this way of relating to the world, much of value beyond the fixation on materialism that powers mainstream culture today in the early twenty-first century.

Postscript

There are two fundamental philosophical viewpoints of human existence, contradictory to one another. The viewpoint with the greatest currency at present in developed countries is that human life is a finite phenomenon hemmed in by time, essentially random, and meaningless. As long ago as the seventeenth century, the English utilitarian philosopher Thomas Hobbes saw human society as the war of all against all. In

Fig. P.I. The women's tradition of cats' cradles and rope dances is a magical act related to threshold patterns and sprite traps.

this viewpoint, human life is no more than a constant struggle, "nasty, brutish, and short." Hobbes was writing at a time when traditional spirituality was questioned as the result of ruthless wars and new technical inventions and the order of the world seemed to be disintegrating. It is clear that this grim and bleak view of existence underlies current materialist doctrines that the accumulation of power and wealth is the sole aim of human life. Politics are based entirely on this destructive utilitarian worldview, with the universal result of conflict and misery. Another way of living is the traditional spiritual view, that human life can be active and purposeful by being integrated with Nature's eternal return. Whether or not this has a religious dimension, the human being is integrated with Nature or Creation, is not an alienated individual. Traditional rites and ceremonies and traditional understandings of our relationship to the eldritch world link individuals into a wider community and through collective action to Nature and the Cosmos.

Bibliography

Adams, William Henry Davenport. 1895. *Witch, Warlock and Magician: Historical Sketches of Magic and Witchcraft in England and Scotland.* London: Chatto and Windus.

Addison, William. 1953. *English Fairs and Markets.* London: Batsford.

Addy, S. O. 1907. "Guising and Mumming in Derbyshire." *The Journal of the Derbyshire Archaeological and Natural History Society* 29: 31–42.

Aldred, Wags. n.d. *Stories from Wags Aldred: Suffolk Stallion Leader.* Helions Bumpstead: Traditions of Suffolk.

Alford, Violet. 1978. *The Hobby Horse and Other Animal Masks.* London: The Merlin Press.

Alger, Ken, Allan Brigham, Brian Hockley, and Julie Wilkingson. 1996. *Cambridge Iron Founders.* Cambridge: Cambridge Industrial Archaeology Society.

Andrews, William. 1898. *Bygone Norfolk.* London: William Andrews.

———, ed. 1899. *Ecclesiastical Curiosities.* London: William Andrews.

Anckorn, Gordon. 1981. *A West Norfolk Camera: King's Lynn, Wells and Wisbech in Old Photographs.* Sevenoaks: Ashgrove Press.

Anonymous. 1850. *Wisbech Hundred.* Wisbech: n.p.

———. 1977. "The Dudley Devil." *Black Country Bugle Annual* 39 (December).

———. Circa 1986. *The Bedford Morris Men.* Bedford: The Bedford Morris Men.

———. Circa 1997. *The King's Lynn May Garland.* King's Lynn: The King's Men.

———. 2001a. "Lords of the Dance." *Hinckley Herald & Journal,* January 10.

———. 2001b. *United Grand Lodge.* London: The United Grand Lodge.

———. 2009. *The Society of the Horseman's Word.* Leicestershire: The Society of Esoteric Endeavour.

Atkinson, Rev. John Christopher. 1891. *Forty Years in a Moorland Parish: Reminiscences and Researches in Danby in Cleveland.* London and New York: Macmillan and Co.

Bales, E. G. 1939. "Folklore from West Norfolk." *Folk-Lore* 50 (March): 66–75.

Barrell, John. 1980. *The Dark Side of the Landscape.* Cambridge: Cambridge University Press.

Barrett, W. H. 1958. "A Cure for Witches." *The East Anglian Magazine,* March, 290–95.

———. 1963. *Tales from the Fens.* London: Routledge and Kegan Paul.

Barrett, W. H., and Enid Porter, eds. 1964. *More Tales from the Fens.* London: Routledge and Kegan Paul.

Bärtsch, Albert. 1993. *Holz Masken. Fastnachts- und Maskenbrauchtum in der Schweiz, in Süddeutschland und Österrech.* Aarau, Switzerland: A. T. Verlag.

Baskervill, Charles Reed. 1924. "'Mummers' Wooing Plays in England." *Modern Philology* 21 (February): 241–45.

Bayliss, Peter. 1997. "Secrets of the Horse Whisperers." *Tradition* 3 (September/October): 12–13.

Bell, Col. A. H. 1965. *Practical Dowsing: A Symposium.* London: G. Bell and Sons.

Bendix, Regina. 1997. *In Search of Authenticity: The Formation of Folklore Studies.* Madison: University of Wisconsin Press.

Bevis, Trevor. 1994. *Wide Horizons: Hard Graft for Old-Time Fenmen.* March Cambridge: Privately published.

Bewick, Thomas. *History of Quadrupeds.* Newcastle upon Tyne: T. Bewick & Son, 1790.

Bird, F. W. 1911. *Memorials of Godmanchester.* Peterborough: Peterborough Advertiser Company.

Blair, John. 2001. *Bampton Folklore.* Whitechurch: Merton Priory Press.

Blomefield, Francis. 1805–1810. *Topographical History of the County of Norfolk.* London: W. Miller.

Bonser, K. J. 1972. *The Drovers.* Newton Abbot: Country Book Club.

Bowles, Bill "Pop." 1986. *The Memoirs of a Fenland Mole Catcher.* Peterborough: Cambridgeshire Libraries Publications.

Boyle, Maurice C. 1983. *Canny Aad Sunlun.* Sunderland: Portsmouth and Sunderland Newspapers PLC.

Brand, John. 1905. *Brand's Popular Antiquities*. London: Reeves and Turner.

Broadwood, Lucy E., and J. A. Fuller Maitland. 1893. *English County Songs*. London and New York: Leadenhall Press.

Bronner, Simon J. 1992. *Creativity and Tradition in Folklore: New Directions*. Logan: Utah State University Press.

Brown, Carleton F., and John George Hohman. 1904. "The Long Hidden Friend." *The Journal of American Folklore* 17 (April–June): 89–152.

Brown, Theo. 1958. "The Black Dog." *Folklore* (September): 175–92.

Bunn, Ivan. 1977. "Black Shuck. Part One: Encounters, Legends and Ambiguities." *Lantern* 18 (Summer): 3–6.

———. 1977. "Black Shuck. Part Two." *Lantern* 19 (Autumn): 4–8.

———. 1982. "A Devil's Shield . . . Notes on Suffolk Witch Bottles." *Lantern* 39 (Autumn): 3–7.

Burgess, Michael W. 1978. "Crossroad and Roadside Burials." *Lantern* 24 (Winter): 6–8.

Burn, Ronald. 1914. "Folk-Lore from Newmarket, Cambridgeshire." *Folklore* 25 (September): 363–66.

Butcher, D. R. 1972. "The Last Ears of Harvest." *The East Anglian Magazine* 31: 463–65.

The Cambridge Chronicle. 1855. January 13, 8.

The Cambridge Independent Press. 1840. January 18, 3.

———. 1851. January 18.

———. 1858. January 16, 7.

———. 1871. January 14, 7.

Cambridge News & Crier. 2010. "Strawberry Fair Wins Licence Fight." March 4, 5.

Canney, Maurice A. 1926. "The Use of Sand in Magic and Religion." *Man*, January, 13.

Caraccioli, Charles. 1772. *An Historical Account of Sturbridge, Bury, and the Most Famous Fairs in Europe and America*. Cambridge: Fletcher and Hodson.

Cawte, Edwin Christopher. 1978. *Ritual Animal Disguise*. London: D. S. Brewer.

Child, Francis James, ed. 1860. *English and Scottish Ballads*. 8 vols. Boston: Little, Brown and Company.

Chumbley, Andrew. 2000. *Grimoire of the Golden Toad*. London: Xoanon Publishing.

————. 2001. *The Leaper between: An Historical Study of the Toad Bone Amulet.* Privately published and circulated.

Cooper, Emmanuel. 1994. *People's Art: Working-Class Art from 1750 to the Present Day.* Edinburgh and London: Mainstream Publishing.

Cooper, Robert L. D. 2006. *Cracking the Freemason's Code.* London: Rider.

Croker, Alec. 1971. *The Crafts of Straw Decoration.* Leicester: Dryad.

Dack, Charles. 1899. *Old Peterborough Customs and Their Survival.* Reprinted from *Journal of the British Archaeological Association* for the Peterborough Natural History, Scientific, and Archaeological Society. London: The Bedford Press.

————. 1911. *Weather and Folk Lore of Peterborough and District.* Peterborough: Peterborough Natural History, Scientific, and Archaeological Society.

Daily News. 1898, July 27.

Dakers, Alan. 1991. *Ticklerton Tale: A History of Eaton-under-Heywood.* Church Stretton: Privately published.

Davidson, Thomas. 1956. "The Horseman's Word: A Rural Initiation Ceremony." *Gwerin* 1: 67–74.

Day, George. 1894. "Notes on Essex Dialect and Folk-Lore, with Some Account of the Divining Rod." *The Essex Naturalist* 8: 71–85.

Defoe, Daniel. 1724. "A Tour Through The Whole Island of Great Britain." London. Vol 1, letter 1 part 3.

De Henley, Walter. 1890. *Le dite de hosebondrie.* London: Longman's, Green, and Company.

Drew, John H. *Transactions of the Birmingham Archaeological Society* 82: 738–43.

Edwards, Maj. T. J. 1961. *Military Customs.* Revised by Arthur L. Kipling. Aldershot: Gale and Polden.

Ellis-Davidson, Hilda. 1993. *The Lost Beliefs of Northern Europe.* London: Routledge.

The Ely Standard. 1937. January 15, 13.

Ettinger, Ellen. 1943. "Documents of British Superstition in Oxford." *Folklore* 54 (March): 227–49.

Evans, E. W. 1961. *The Miners of South Wales.* Cardiff: University of Wales Press.

Evans, George Ewart. 1965. *Ask the Fellows Who Cut the Hay.* London: Faber and Faber.

————. 1966. *The Pattern Under the Plough.* London: Faber and Faber.

————. 1971. *The Pattern under the Plough*. London: Faber and Faber (new edition).

Farmer, Henry George. 1950. *Military Music*. New York: Chanticleer.

Flaherty, Robert Pearson. 1992. "Todaustragen, the Ritual Expulsion of Death at Mid-Lent: History and Scholarship." *Folklore* 103: 40–55.

Forby, Robert. 1830. *The Vocabulary of East Anglia*. 2 vols. London: J. B. Nichols and Son.

Frampton, George. 1991. *More Honoured in the Breach than in the Observance: Plough Monday Customs of Cambridgeshire, Past and Present*. Manuscript.

————. 1993. *Pity the Poor Ploughboy—Balsham's Plough Monday*. Tonbridge: Privately published.

————. 1994. *Necessary to Keep Up the Day: Plough Monday and Musical Tradition in Little Downham*. Tonbridge: Privately published.

————. 1996. *Vagrants, Rogues and Vagabonds: Plough Monday Tradition in Old Huntingdonshire and the Soke of Peterborough*. Tonbridge: Privately published.

Francis, Hywel. 1976. "South Wales." In *The General Strike: 1926*, edited by Jeffrey Skelley. London: Lawrence and Wishart.

Frazer, J. G. 1897. "Plough Monday at Witchford, Isle of Ely." *Folk-Lore* 1: 184.

Frazer, J. G., and G. C. Moore Smith. 1909. "Straw Bear Tuesday." *Folk-Lore* 20 (June): 202–3.

Frazer, Sir James. 1931. "Straw Bear at Jena." *Folk-Lore* 42 (March): 87.

Friedman, Jonathan. 1992. "The Past in the Future: History and the Politics of Identity." *American Anthropologist* 94: 837–59.

Gailey, Alan. 1974. "Chapbook Influence on Irish Mummers' Plays." *Folklore* 85 (Spring): 1–22.

The Gentleman's Magazine. 1754. 16–17.

Gerish, William Blythe. 1911. *The Folk-Lore of Hertfordshire*. Hertfordshire: Bishop's Stortford.

Glanvil, Joseph. 1689. *Sadducismus Triumphatus, or Full and Plain Evidence Concerning Witches and Apparitions*. London: n.p.

Glover, Janet R. 1960. *The Story of Scotland*. London: Faber.

Glyde, John, Jr. 2008. *Norfolk Garland: A Collection of the Superstitious Beliefs and Practices, Proverbs, Curious Customs, Ballads and Songs of the People of Norfolk, as Well as Anecdotes Illustrative of the Genius or Peculiarities of Norfolk Celebrities*. London: Jarrold and Sons.

Goodman, Neville, and Albert Goodman. 1882. *A Handbook of Fen Skating.* London: Sampson Low, Marston, Searle, and Rivington.

Griffinhoofe, H. G. 1894. "Breeding Stone." *The Essex Review* III: 144.

Gurdon, Lady Camilla. 1892. "Folk-Lore from South-East Suffolk." *Folk-Lore* 3 (December): 558—60.

———. 1893. *County Folk-Lore: Suffolk.* London: David Butt.

Gutch, Mrs. Eliza, and Mabel Peacock. 1908. *Examples of Printed Folk-Lore Concerning Lincolnshire.* London: David Nutt.

Gwyn. 1999. *Light from the Shadows: A Mythos of Modern Witchcraft.* Berks, UK: Chieveley.

Hadow, Grace E., and Ruth Anderson. 1924. "Scraps of English Folk-Lore IX (Suffolk)." *Folk-Lore* 35 (December): 346–60.

Hamill, John. 1986. *The Craft: A History of English Freemasonry.* London: Crucible.

Harland, M. G., and H. J. Harland. 1980. *The Flooding of Eastern England.* Peterborough: Minimax Books, Deeping St. James.

Hart, A. Tindal. 1962. *Country Counting House: The Story of Two Eighteenth Century Clerical Account Books.* London: Phoenix.

Heanley, Rev. R. M. 1902. "The Vikings: Traces of their Folklore in Marshland." *Saga Book of the Viking Club. Part 1* III (January).

Hennels, C. E. 1972. "The Wild Herb Men." *The East Anglian Magazine* 32: 79–80.

Hissey, J. J. 1898. *Over Fen and Wold.* London: Macmillan.

Hobsbawm, Eric, and George Rudé. 1969. *Captain Swing.* London: Lawrence and Wishart.

Holmes, J. G. January 1952. "Plough Monday Plays." *Nottinghamshire Countryside* 13: 7–8.

Hone, William. 1827. *The Every-Day Book: or, Everlasting Calendar of Popular Amusements, Sports, Pastimes, Ceremonies, Manners, Customs and Events.* 2 vols. London: Hunt and Clarke.

Howe, Bea. 1952. "Witches over the Crouch." *The East Anglian Magazine,* November, 21–24.

———. 1956. "James Murrell, Last of the Essex Wizards." *The East Anglian Magazine,* January, 138–41.

Howson, John, collector. 1992. *Songs Sung in Suffolk.* Haughley: Veteran Tapes.

————. 1993. *Many a Good Horseman: A Survey of Traditional Music Making in Mid Suffolk.* Haughley: Veteran Tapes.

Howson, Katie. 2005. "English Traditional Music from East Anglia." *English Dance and Song* 67 (Winter): 18–20.

Hudleston, N. A. n.d. *Lore and Laughter of South Cambridgeshire.* Cambridge: St. Tibbs Press.

Hughes, Philip Gwyn. 1943. *Wales and the Drovers.* London: Foyle's Welsh Company.

Humphreys, John. 1995. *More Tales of the Old Poachers.* Newton Abbot: David and Charles.

Jakes, Chris. 2004. *Britain in Old Photographs: Cambridge.* Stroud: Budding Books.

J. B. 1886. "Superstitions and Customs of Leicestershire." *The Nottingham Guardian,* January 13, 3.

Jekyll, Gertrude. 1904. *Old West Surrey.* London: Longmans, Green and Company.

Jobson, Allan. 1966. *A Suffolk Calendar.* London: Robert Hale.

Johnson, Walter. 1912. *Byways in Archaeology.* Cambridge: Cambridge University Press.

Jonas, M. C., J. B. Partridge, Ella M. Leather, and F. S. Potter. 1913. "Scraps of English Folk-Lore." *Folk-Lore* 24 (July): 234–51.

Jones, Prudence. 1979. "Broomsticks." *Albion* 4: 8–10.

Jones-Baker, Doris. 1977. *The Folklore of Hertfordshire.* London: B. T. Batsford Ltd.

Keynes, Florence A. 1950. *Gathering Up the Threads.* Cambridge: W. Heffer and Sons Ltd.

"The King of the Norfolk Poachers." 1974. In *I Walked by Night,* edited by Lilias Rider Haggard. Woodbridge: Boydell Press.

Knight, Charles. 1859. *The Popular History of England: An Illustrated History of Society.* London: Bradbury and Evans.

Lake, Jeremy. 1989. *Historic Farm Buildings.* London: Blandford.

Lambert, Margaret, and Enid Marx. 1989. *English Popular Art.* London: Merlin Press.

Langley, Tom. n.d. *The Tipton Slasher, His Life and Times.* Halesowen: The Black Country Society.

Larwood, Jacob, and John Camden Hotten. 1908. *The History of Signboards from the Earliest Times to the Present Day.* London: Chatto & Windus.

Laver, Henry. 1889. "Fifty Years Ago in Essex." *The Essex Naturalist* III (January–June): 27–35.

Leather, Ella Mary. 1912. *The Folk-Lore of Herefordshire*. Hereford: Jakeman and Carver; London: Sidgwick and Jackson.

Lee, Rev. Frederick George, ed. 1875. *Glimpses of the Supernatural*. 2 vols. London: Henry S. King and Co.

Leeds Mercury. 1728. June 11.

Leland, John. 1770. *Collectanea*. Edited by Thomas Hearne. London: Impensis Gul and Jo Richardson.

The Lincoln, Rutland and Stamford Mercury. 1821. January 22.

———. 1864. January 15.

Lugh. 1982. *"Old George" Pickingill and the Roots of Modern Witchcraft*. London: Wiccan Publications.

Mackinnon, John. 1881. *Account of Messingham in the County of Lincoln (1825)*. Edited by Edward Peacock. Privately printed.

MacPherson, J. M. 1929. *Primitive Beliefs in the North East of Scotland*. London: Longmans, Green and Company.

Maple, Eric. 1960. "The Witches of Canewdon." *Folklore* 71 (December): 241–50.

———. 1965. "Witchcraft and Magic in the Rochford Hundred." *Folklore* 76 (Autumn): 213–24.

Marshall, Sybil. 1967. *Fenland Chronicle*. Cambridge: Cambridge University Press.

Massey, Alan. 1999. "The Reigate Witch Bottle." *Current Archaeology* 169: 34–36.

McAldowie, Alex. 1896. "Personal Experiences in Witchcraft." *Folk-Lore* 7 (September): 309–14.

McIntosh, Tania. 1998. *The Decline of Stourbridge Fair, 1770–1934*. Leicester: University of Leicester.

McNeill, F. Marian. 1957–68. *The Silver Bough*. 4 vols. Glasgow: William Maclellan.

Merrifield, Ralph. 1954. "The Use of Bellarmines and Witch Bottles." *The Guildhall Miscellany* 3.

M. G. C. H. 1936. "On a Hardle." *The East Anglian Magazine*, June, 507.

Miles, Clarence Francis. 1936. *The History and Romance of "Rattling" Musical Jaw Bones*. Worcester, Mass.: Privately printed.

Miller, William Marion. 1944. "How to Become a Witch." *The Journal of American Folklore* 57 (October–December): 280.

Mitchell, Ena. 1985. *Notes on the History of Four Cambridge Commons.* Cambridge: n.p.

Molloy, Pat. 1983. *And They Blessed Rebecca: An Account of the Welsh Toll-Gate Riots 1839–1844.* Llandysul: Gomer Press.

Mortimer, Bishop Robert. 1972. *Exorcism: The Report of a Commission Convened by the Bishop of Exeter.* Edited by Dom Robert Petitpierre. London: The Society for Promoting Christian Knowledge.

Neat, Timothy. 2002. *The Horseman's Word.* Edinburgh: Birlinn.

Needham, Joseph, and Arthur L. Peck. 1933. "Molly Dancing in East Anglia." *Journal of the English Folk Dance and Song Society* 1 (2):79–95.

Newell, Joe. 1991. *The Holywell Story.* Cambridge: Graham-Cameron Publishing.

Newman, Leslie F. 1940. "Notes on Some Rural and Trade Initiations in the Eastern Counties." *Folk-Lore* 51 (March): 32–42.

———. 1946. "Some Notes on the Practise of Witchcraft in the Eastern Counties." *Folk-Lore* 57 (March): 12–33.

———. 1948. "Some Notes on the Pharmacology and Therapeutic Value of Folk-Medicines." *Folklore* 59 (September): 118–35.

The News Chronicle. 1947. January 6.

Nichols, J. 1786. *The History and Antiquities of Barnwell Abbey and Sturbridge Fair.* London: Bibliotheca Topographica Britannica.

Olsen, Olaf. 1966. *Hørg, Hof of Kirke.* Copenhagen: University of Copenhagen.

O'Neill, John. 1895. "Straw." *The Journal of American Folk-Lore* 8 (October–December): 291–98.

Ord, John. 1920. "The Most Secret of Secret Societies: Ancient Scottish Horsemen." *The Glasgow Weekly Herald,* November 13.

———. [1930] 1995. *Ord's Bothy Songs and Ballads of Aberdeen Banff and Moray Angus and the Mearns.* Reprint, Edinburgh: John Donald Publishers. Citations refer to the original edition.

Palmer, Roy. 1992. *Folklore of Hereford and Worcester.* Woonton Almeley: Logaston Press.

Parsons, Catherine E. 1915. "Notes on Cambridgeshire Witchcraft." *Proceedings of the Cambridge Antiquarian Society* XIX: 31–52.

———. 1952. *Horseheath: Some Recollections of a Cambridgeshire Parish.* Little Abingdon: Typescript.

Pattinson, G. W. 1953. "Adult Education and Folklore." *Folklore* 64 (September): 424–26.

Peacock, Edward. 1877. *A Glossary of Words Used in the Wapentakes of Manley and Corringham, Lincolnshire.* London: The Dialect Society.

Peacock, Mabel Geraldine W. 1901. "The Folk-Lore of Lincolnshire." *Folk-Lore* 12 (June): 161–80.

———. 1907. "The Fifth of November and Guy Fawkes." *Folk-Lore* 18 (December): 449–50.

Pennick, Nigel. 1970. "East Anglian Wooden Architecture." *Cambridge Voice,* series 2: 8–9.

———. 1985. *Daddy Witch and Old Mother Redcap.* Cambridge: Cornerstone Press.

———. 1986. *Skulls, Cats and Witch Bottles.* Bar Hill: Nigel Pennick Editions.

———. [1995] 2004. *Secrets of East Anglian Magic.* London: Robert Hale. Second edition, Milverton: Capall Bann Publishing.

———. 1996. *Celtic Sacred Landscapes.* London and New York: Thames and Hudson.

———. 1998. *Crossing the Borderlines: Guising, Masking & Ritual Animal Disguises in the European Tradition.* Milverton: Capall Bann Publishing.

———. 1999a. *Beginnings: Geomancy, Builders' Rites and Electional Astrology in the European Tradition.* Milverton: Capall Bann Publishing.

———. 1999b. "Regarding the Ooser." *3rd Stone* 35 (July–September): 39–40.

———. 2002a. *Masterworks: Arts and Crafts of Traditional Buildings in Northern Europe.* Wymeswold: Heart of Albion Press.

———. 2002b. *The Power Within: The Way of the Warrior and the Martial Arts in the European Tradition.* Milverton: Capall Bann Publishing.

———. 2003. "Postmoderne Monumente." *Hagia Chora* 17: 109.

———. 2003–04. "Heathen Holy Places in Northern Europe: A Cultural Overview." *TYR: Myth-Culture-Tradition* 2: 139–49.

———. 2005a. "A Black and White Issue?" *English Dance and Song* 67 (Autumn): 30.

———. 2005b. "Erloschenes Urheberrecht." *Hagia Chora* 22: 72.

———. 2005c. "Vom Fortbestehen alter Grenzen." *Hagia Chora* 20: 103.

———. 2006a. *The Eldritch World.* Earl Shilton: Lear Books.

———. 2006b. *Folk-Lore of East Anglia and Adjoining Counties.* Bar Hill: Spiritual Arts & Crafts Publishing.

———. Circa 2010a. *The Toadman.* Leicestershire: The Society of Esoteric Endeavour.

———. (2010b) 2019. *Wyrdstaves of the North*. Earl Shilton: Lear Books. New edition published under the title *Runic Lore and Legend*, Rochester, Vt.: Destiny Books.

———. 2015. *Pagan Magic of the Northern Tradition*. Rochester, Vt.: Destiny Books.

———. 2017. *Curious Journies*. Kindle.

Pennick, Nigel, and Helen Field. 2003. *A Book of Beasts*. Milverton: Capall Bann Publishing.

The Peterborough Advertiser. 1873. January 18, 3.

The Peterborough Advertiser, 1886, January 16.

———. 1888. January 14, 5.

———. 1927. January 14.

The Peterborough and Huntingdonshire Standard. 1894. January 13, 8.

The Peterborough Standard. 1899. March 11.

Pittaway, Andy, and Bernard Scofield. 1976a. *The Complete Country Bizarre*. London: Astragal.

———. 1976b. *Country Bazaar: A Handbook of Country Pleasures*. London: Fontana.

Porteous, Crichton. 1976. *The Ancient Customs of Derbyshire*. Derby: Derbyshire Countryside.

Porter, Enid. 1958. "Some Folk Life of the Fens." *Folklore* 69 (June): 112–22.

———. 1961. "Folk Life and Traditions in the Fens." *Folklore* 72 (December): 584–98.

———. 1969. *Cambridgeshire Customs and Folklore*. Fenland material provided by W. H. Barrett. London: Routledge and Kegan Paul.

———. 1974. *The Folklore of East Anglia*. London: Batsford.

Putterill, John "Reverend Jack." n.d. *Conrad Noel: Prophet and Priest*. Transcription of radio broadcast, n.p.

———. 1950. "The Folk Dances of Thaxted." *The East Anglian Magazine* 9: 340–42.

Randall, Arthur. 1966. *Sixty Years a Fenman*. Edited by Enid Porter. London: Routledge and Kegan Paul.

Rayson, George. 1865a. "East Anglian Folk-Lore, no. 1. 'Weather Proverbs.'" *The East Anglian, or, Notes & Queries on Subjects Connected with the Counties of Suffolk, Cambridgeshire, Essex and Norfolk* I: 155–62.

———. 1865b. "East Anglian Folk-Lore, no. 2 'Omens.'" *The East Anglian,* or, *Notes & Queries on Subjects Connected with the Counties of Suffolk, Cambridgeshire, Essex and Norfolk* I: 185–86.

———. 1865c. "East Anglian Folk-Lore, no. 3 'Charms.'" *The East Anglian, or, Notes & Queries on Subjects Connected with the Counties of Suffolk, Cambridgeshire, Essex and Norfolk* I: 214–17.

Ridley, Matt. 1996. *The Origins of Virtue.* London: Penguin Books.

Robbins, Rossell Hope. 1963. "The Imposture of Witchcraft." *Folklore* 74 (Winter): 545–62.

Roper, Charles. 1883. "On Witchcraft Superstition in Norfolk." *Harper's New Monthly Magazine* 87 (October): 792–97.

Ross, Frederick. 1892. *Bygone London.* London: Hutchinson.

Rudkin, Ethel H. 1933. "Lincolnshire Folk-Lore." *Folk-Lore* 44 (September): 279–95.

———. 1936. *Lincolnshire Folklore.* London: Gainsborough.

Sandford, Lettice. 1983. *Straw Work and Corn Dollies.* London: Batsford.

Saunders, W. H. Bernard. 1888. *Legends and Traditions of Huntingdonshire.* London: Simpkin Marshall, Elliot Stock.

Schofield, Derek. 2005. "A Black and White Issue?' *English Dance and Song* 67 (Summer): 12–14.

Scott, Sir Walter. 2009. *Letters on Demonology and Witchcraft.* Radford, Va.: Wilder Publications.

———. 2018. "The Two Drovers." www.walterscott.lib.ed.ac.uk/etexts/etexts /twodrovers_1751.htm.

Simper, Robert. 1980. *Traditions of East Anglia.* Woodbridge: The Boydell Press.

———. Circa 2000. *Rivers to the Fens.* English Estuaries Series, vol. 8. Lavenham, Suffolk: Creekside Publishing.

Singer, William. 1881. *An Exposition of the Miller and Horseman's Word, or the True System of Raising the Devil.* Aberdeen: James Daniel.

Smedley, Norman. 1955. "Two Bellarmine Bottles from Coddenham." *Proceedings of the Suffolk Institute of Archæology* XXVI: 229.

Smith, Georgina. 1981. "Chapbooks and Traditional Plays: Communication and Performance." *Folklore* 92: 196–202.

The Society of the Horseman's Grip and Word. 2009. London: The Society of Esoteric Endeavour.

S. R. 1614. *The Art of Jugling or Legerdemain.* London: George Eld.

Starsmore, I. 1975. *English Fairs.* London: Thames and Hudson.

Sternberg, Thomas. 1851. *The Dialect and Folk-Lore of Northamptonshire.* London: John Russell Smith.

Sturt, George. 1927. *A Farmer's Life.* London: Jonathan Cape.

"Superstition in the West Highlands." 1877. *Notes & Queries* 186 (July 21): 163.

Taylor, Alison. 1999. *Cambridge: The Hidden History.* Stroud: Tempus Publishing.

Taylor, John. 2006. *The Old Order and the New: P. H. Emerson and Photography 1885–1895.* Munich, Berlin, London, and New York: Prestel.

Taylor, Mark R. 1929. "Norfolk Folk-Lore." *Folk-Lore* 40 (June): 113–33.

Tebbutt, C. F. 1941. *History of Bluntisham cum Earith.* Bluntisham: Privately published.

———. 1942. "Huntingdonshire Folk and Their Folklore." *Transactions of the Cambridgeshire and Huntingdonshire Archaeological Society* VI: 119–54.

———. 1950. "Huntingdonshire Folk and Their Folklore." *Transactions of the Cambridgeshire and Huntingdonshire Archaeological Society:* VII: 54–64.

———. 1984. *Huntingdonshire Folklore.* St. Ives: Norris Museum.

Thakeray, William M. 1848. *Vanity Fair.* Leipzig: Bernhard Tauchnitz.

The Times. 1917. March 5.

Toulson, Shirley. 1980. *The Drovers.* Shire Album 45. Princes Risborough: Shire Publications Ltd.

Tregelles, J. A. 1908. *A History of Hoddesdon in the County of Hertfordshire.* Hertford: Stephen Austin & Sons.

Tuke, John. 1801. *A General View of the Agriculture of the North Riding of Yorkshire.* York: Board of Agriculture.

Wales, F. L. 1920. *The History of the Shelfords—Great and Little.* Great Shelford: Manuscript.

Webster, D., ed. 1820. *Collection of Rare and Curious Tracts on Witchcraft.* Edinburgh: T. Webster.

Wentworth-Day, James. 1973. *Essex Ghosts.* Bourne End: Spurbooks.

Wheeler, William Henry. 1868. *History of the Fens of South Lincolnshire.* Boston: J. M. Newcomb.

Widnall, Samuel Page. 1875. *History of Grantchester.* Grantchester: Privately published.

———. 1892. *Gossiping through the Streets of Cambridge.* Grantchester: Privately Published.

Wortley, Russell. 1972. *Traditional Music in and around Cambridge.* Unpublished typescript.

Wright, A. R., and W. Aldis Wright. 1912. "Seventeenth-Century Cures and Charms." *Folk-Lore* 23 (December): 490–97.

Wright, Authur Robinson, and Thomas East Lones. 1936. *British Calendar Customs I. Movable Festivals.* London: William Glaisher Ltd.

———. 1938. *British Calendar Customs II. Fixed Festivals, January–May, Inclusive.* London: William Glaisher Ltd.

———. 1940. *British Calendar Customs III Fixed Festivals, June–December, Inclusive.* London: William Glaisher Ltd.

Index